JavaScript

Addison-Wesley
Nitty Gritty

PROGRAMMING SERIES

JavaScript

Elmar Dellwig   Ingo Dellwig

ADDISON-WESLEY

An imprint of Pearson Education

Boston • San Francisco • New York • Toronto • Montreal • London • Munich
Paris • Madrid • Cape Town • Sydney • Tokyo • Singapore • Mexico City

PEARSON EDUCATION LIMITED

Head Office
Edinburgh Gate, Harlow, Essex CM20 2JE
Tel: +44 (0)1279 623623 Fax: +44 (0)1279 431059

London Office
128 Long Acre, London WC2E 9AN
Tel: +44 (0)20 7447 2000 Fax: +44 (0)20 7240 5771
Websites:
www.it-minds.com   www.aw.com/cseng

First published in Great Britain 2002
© Pearson Education Limited 2002

First published in 2000 as *JavaScript 1.3 Nitty-Gritty* by Addison-Wesley
Verlag, Germany.

Library of Congress Cataloguing Publication Data
Applied for.

British Library Cataloguing in Publication Data
A CIP catalogue record for this book can be obtained from the British Library.

ISBN 0-201-75875-X

10 9 8 7 6 5 4 3 2 1

Translated and typeset by Berlitz GlobalNET (UK) Ltd. of Luton, Bedfordshire.
Printed and bound in Great Britain by Biddles Ltd. of Guildford and King's Lynn.

The publishers' policy is to use paper manufactured from sustainable forests.

Contents

Part III – Go ahead!   205

Dear Reader,

The Internet continues to develop at a rapid pace. Modern homepages are no longer static sources of information and now offer genuine interactivity. Active Internet pages of this kind cannot be implemented by just using HTML, the main language in the World Wide Web. That's why you have already taken a step in the right direction by buying this book on JavaScript.

You will get to know the key principles of JavaScript programming and will be able to use the quick reference guide to extend your knowledge to expert level. Afterwards you can check out the tips and tricks section to find out how to get more information about JavaScript.

At this point we would like to thank all those who contributed (in whatever way) to the creation of this book:

Firstly, our thanks go to our editor at Addison-Wesley, Christina Gibbs, who pulled out all the stops to allow us more time to write this book.

Thanks also to our parents and friends who hardly ever caught sight of us during the "white-hot" creative phase. We're sorry but things will calm down again now – promise!

Last but not least, I (Ingo Dellwig) would like to thank the members of the Dortmund University Orchestra for being so thoughtful when I was immersed in my writing during our concert tour of Tuscany. Once again it was great fun touring with the orchestra.

We hope that you enjoy this book and that you will find in it all the information you need about JavaScript.

Elmar and Ingo Dellwig
Werne, July 2000

Elmar and Ingo Dellwig

... are brothers and are the first port of call for their friends when it comes to questions about computers, the Internet or programming.

Elmar Dellwig (right)

... is making his debut as an author with this book. He has been a computer enthusiast since the days of the C 64 – something that has come in useful during his training as an Information Technology tutor. While studying Computer Science at the Technical College in Dortmund, he also worked as a hotliner for an international online services provider. This greatly expanded his knowledge of Internet-related issues. Encouraged by his brother, he has now been drawn to writing books.

Ingo Dellwig (left)

... is an enthusiastic and dedicated Internet user who has already had his own homepage for several years. He has been working with computers since as early as 1986. His part-time work on the hotline of a major online service provider enabled him to gather experience with the Internet, while at the same time completing his Computer Studies course at the University of Dortmund. During this time, he was frequently confronted with the problems encountered by users in creating their own homepages. He became self-employed in 1997 and founded SPECTROsoftware, a software house that creates homepages for companies in a variety of industries, as well as working on projects in the entertainment sector and providing training courses. At this point he also published his first book on homepages, which was to be followed by numerous titles covering various aspects of the Internet, hardware and programming.

Part I

Start up!

Introduction 1

This section will introduce you to the JavaScript language and also take a look at good programming practice. We will discuss some issues on the basis of examples and will provide you with a quick reference guide in the next section. This contains all the information you will need to develop complex JavaScripts. The third section contains additional suggestions and tips that will show you a few tricks for turning good JavaScript into something special.

1.1 Requirements

JavaScript is a programming language used in the Internet – or more precisely in the "World Wide Web" (WWW). This kind of script is usually embedded in an HTML text. "HTML" stands for "Hypertext Markup Language" and is the standard language used on the WWW. HTML files (and therefore Java-Script programs too) consist of normal text. This is why a simple text editor is all you need to program JavaScript. Naturally we also want to see the results of our work. For this we need a "WWW browser". Both programs must fulfill a number of requirements, as listed below.

> **Tip** Because the files have to be stored somewhere and we don't want to spend a long time searching around, please create a folder called "JS13" in your home directory. All JavaScript files will be stored here.

1.1.1 Browsers

Because no one would want to read HTML or JavaScript source text directly, the first thing we need is an interpreter. The program used for this is called a browsser. This type of program reads the source text line-by-line and performs the instructs contained there. Sometimes it's just text that needs to be displayed, but it is becoming more common for images to be loaded and displayed. Another key function of the browser is to execute your command when you want to load another page as suggested by the current page. The browser also translates and runs JavaScript programs. In other words, it operates as a compiler for JavaScript.

Tip You can download current browser versions from the Internet. For more information on this topic, please see Appendix C.

There are lots of different browsers and their quality can vary. The most primitive of them all is "LYNX". This is purely a text browser. In other words you cannot use it to display graphics. This program cannot handle JavaScript either. For this reason it is useless for our purposes. However, just remember that there are still some users out there who cannot use better quality browsers because these do not run on old computers. These users will not be able to enjoy your scripts. We will point out some alternatives for these users in this book.

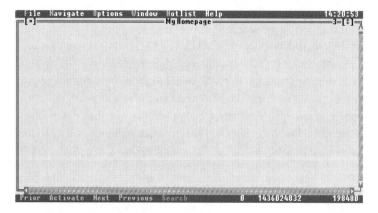

Figure 1.1 *The oldest browser we could find is called LYNX*

Next on our list is Mosaic. Although this program can work with graphics, it is also unable to handle JavaScript.

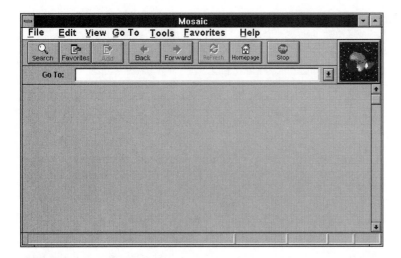

Figure 1.2 *Mosaic is also unsuitable for JavaScript programming*

For this reason we advise you to use either Netscape Navigator, Netscape Communicator or Microsoft Internet Explorer. If you can get hold of a copy of Netscape Navigator 4.06 or Internet Explorer 5.0 you will have everything you need to work through this book.

JavaScript Version	100% compatible	not 100% compatible
JavaScript 1.0	Navigator 2.0	Microsoft Internet Explorer 3.x
JavaScript 1.1	Navigator 3.0	Opera 3.x
JavaScript 1.2	Navigator 4.0–4.05	Microsoft Internet Explorer 4.x
JavaScript 1.3	Navigator 4.06–4.73	Microsoft Internet Explorer 5.x

Table 1.1 *Which browsers support which JavaScript versions?*

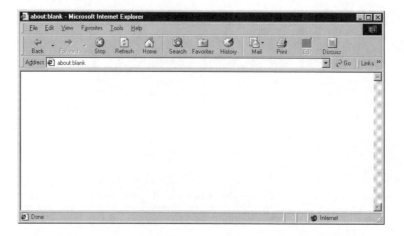

Figure 1.3 *Microsoft Internet Explorer (in this case version 5.0) is the one most suitable for our needs*

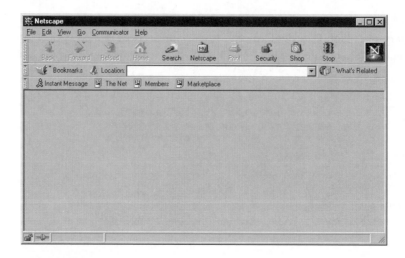

Figure 1.4 *Netscape Navigator (in this case version 4.7) is also suitable for JavaScript*

1.1.2   Text editor

Somehow we need to tell the computer how the JavaScript homepage is to look. All this requires is a simple text editor. For example, if you are using Windows as your operating system, you will already have the "Notepad" editor. You will find this in the ACCESSORIES program folder or under START / PROGRAMS / ACCESSORIES / EDITOR in Windows 95/98.

If you prefer to use another editor, make sure you save your file as text only. In the case of a Word file saved in .doc format, format control characters are saved as well as your HTML text. These cannot be handled by the browser and make the file useless for our purposes. Here's an example:

```
<HTML>
<BODY>
TEST
</BODY>
</HTML>
```

This source text should eventually display the word TEST on the screen. The meaning of the various commands will be explained later. If you save this file in Word in .doc format, then the source text will look like this:

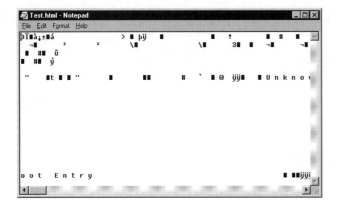

Figure 1.5 *The source text is unrecognizable ...*

If we now look at the page in the browser, we will also see something very interesting, but this has nothing to do with the source text we have keyed in:

Figure 1.6 *... this result is not very satisfactory either*

We will explain how to avoid mistakes like this later on. The important point for the moment is that you should choose a text editor that can save normal text without control characters.

1.2 Crash course in HTML

We have already told you that JavaScripts are embedded in an HTML file. For this reason we should quickly familiarize ourselves with the key terms in this language.

HTML is extremely transparent. It simply involves writing text whose appearance is defined by tags. In addition you can also integrate images, tables and multimedia elements. Let's get down to business.

1.2.1 Creating an HTML page

Open your editor and create a new text file. Because you want the computer to interpret this file as an HTML page later on, we need to identify it in two ways. Firstly the text must begin with <HTML> and end with </HTML>.

Because you are probably wondering what the brackets mean, we should tell you that you have just encountered the first tag. In most cases there is a start tag and an end tag. The end tag only differs from the start tag by a slash. The full text between the <HTML> tag and the </HTML> end tag is interpreted as HTML language. So, please enter the following lines:

```
<HTML>
</HTML>
```

You can now save this file so that it will be available on the hard disk. This is where the second identifier comes in, because all HTML files must end in .HTM or .HTML. Because not all operating systems accept four characters after the dot, it is best to use the extension .HTM. Now save the file under the name index.htm in your JS13 folder.

Why did we call the file index? Simple: If there are several HTML files in a subfolder, the browser will always select the file named index.htm if you do not specify another file name. If you called up this file now, you wouldn't see very much because up to now all the computer knows is that the content of the file is HTML.

1.2.2 Head and body

To bring a bit of life into your page it wouldn't be a bad idea to enter some text. But before you start, there's one more thing you should know: HTML pages can be divided into two parts. The first part is called the head and is indicated by the tag <HEAD>. Because the head encompasses an area, there is also a closing tag </HEAD>. Everything contained in the head of the HTML page will not be displayed directly on the page, but will make itself known in another way. For example, you should choose a title for your homepage. In most browsers, this is displayed in the title bar next to the browser name. The title is indicated by the marker <TITLE>.

Because the page would still be empty – after all the title does not appear on every page – and every head needs a body, we should add the marker <BODY>. Everything entered in the body usually appears on the page. This means you can add to your text.

```
<HTML>
<HEAD>
<TITLE>TEST</TITLE>
```

```
</HEAD>
<BODY>
Test: OK
</BODY>
</HTML>
```

Now we should take a look at our results. Save this text again in `index.htm` and start your browser. It has become standard practice for the upper part of the browser to contain a text field called "URL:", "Address:" or "Go:". This is where you enter the details of the page you want to see. Because your new HTML page is still on the hard disk, you can open it by entering `file:///c:/js13/index.htm`. Of course if you have chosen a different folder or drive during the preparations, you should change the command as necessary. Press Enter to confirm your entry. The following information will be displayed:

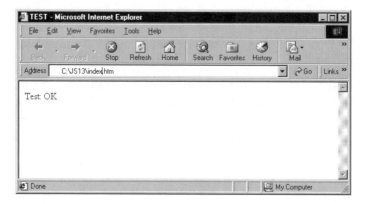

Figure 1.7 *The page header and the text displayed are exactly what we expected*

If the file is not displayed or you get an error then choose "Open" from the File menu and navigate to the file within the file browser. Alternatively, you can double-click on the document you have created to open it in your browser.

You have now created and displayed your first HTML page. The layout still looks a bit meager. You could use what you have already learned to display texts in a browser, but still need a few important markers that can make the text easier to read. The first marker we'll introduce is the `<SCRIPT>` tag. This is very useful for our purposes.

1.2.3 The <SCRIPT> tag

Script languages are identified by the <SCRIPT> tag. JavaScript is an example of a script language. That's why we use <SCRIPT> to distinguish JavaScript text from HTML source code. Here's an example:

```
<HTML>
<HEAD>
  <SCRIPT LANGUAGE="JavaScript">
    <!--
    function getname(str) {
    alert("Hello, "+ str + "!");
    }
    -->
  </SCRIPT>
</HEAD>
<BODY>
  Please enter your name:
  <FORM>
    <INPUT TYPE="text" NAME="name"
      ONBLUR="getname(this.value)" VALUE="">
  </FORM>
</BODY>
</HTML>
```

Save this source text as query.htm and take a look at the result in the browser:

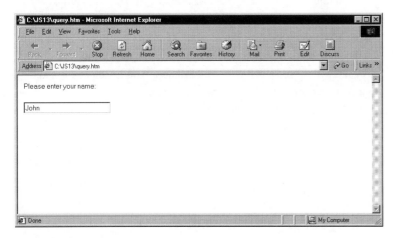

Figure 1.8 *How the test script looks in the browser*

Enter your name in the input field and press (↵). The following window appears:

Figure 1.9 *The JavaScript has completed its task*

What we are getting at is the fact that it was the `<SCRIPT LANGUAGE="Java-Script">` line that allowed us to use JavaScript. As we said before, other script languages can also be controlled with `<SCRIPT>`. The attribute `LANGUAGE` is needed to enable the browser to recognize which language is being used. Attributes can link values to tags. So `LANGUAGE` is assigned the value `"JavaScript"`. Because the attribute is within the tag, it is clear that this script is written in JavaScript. We will not deal with the other tags and attributes in the source text or with the script itself at this point. Try to be patient. It is much more interesting at this point to find out what other attributes can be used in `<SCRIPT>`:

Attribute	Description
CHARSET	This attribute specifies which character set is to be used for the script. The standard setting is ISO-8859-1.
DEFER	This attribute occurs all by itself and therefore does not need to be assigned a value. If this attribute is set, the browser is notified that the script does not generate any on-screen data.
EVENT	This indicates the event the script was written for. More about this later.
FOR	This specifies which element is linked to this event script. This too will be explained later.
LANGUAGE	As explained, this attribute indicates the language used for the script.
SRC	An external data source can be accessed here. This can be useful if, for example, lots of HTML files use the same script.
TYPE	This attribute indicates the MIME type of the script source code.

Table 1.2 *The attributes of* `<SCRIPT>`

Tip You will find more tags listed in the "Tips and tricks" section.

1.3 The basics of JavaScript

This section will introduce you to JavaScript. It will explain how to write, save and run your first script. After this you will learn how to store data in variables and how to use these variables. But before we get too carried away, let's start with an example.

1.3.1 Hello World!

It is traditional for the first program in a new programming language to greet the world. That's why we are going to display the banner `Hello World!` on the screen. When you see these words displayed, you will have successfully generated and executed your first program. Let's get to work ...

Start your favorite text editor and enter the following lines.

```
<HTML>
<SCRIPT LANGUAGE="JavaScript">
  document.write("Hello World!");
</SCRIPT>
</HTML>
```

As you already know, the `<HTML>` tag marks the HTML part of the document. To tell the browser that we have programmed a JavaScript, we must include the `<SCRIPT>` tag. The actual source text of the script appears between `<SCRIPT>` and `</SCRIPT>`. Because all we want to do is to insert the words `Hello World!` into the HTML document by means of a JavaScript, we simply call up the `write` function in the `document` class. We then just assign the two words to this. Later on you will find out exactly what we mean by classes and functions. We'll also look at the syntax in detail. For the moment, just take our word for it that the `document.write("Hello World!");` line has precisely this effect.

To see the result, we have to save the source text to the hard disk. If you haven't done so already, please create a folder named `JS13` on your hard disk. Then save our first script in a file named `HelloWorld.html`.

> **Tip** Remember that the source text must be saved in text format. If you save a script in Word format for example, additional control characters will be saved that will make an HTML file useless.

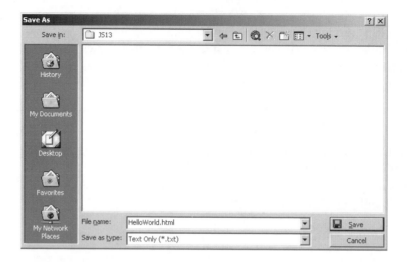

Figure 1.10 *HTML files should always be saved in text format*

Our masterpiece is now located on your hard disk. But what does the result look like? If you have installed an Internet browser – such as Microsoft Internet Explorer or Netscape Communicator – you can open your file using the explorer by simply double-clicking on it.

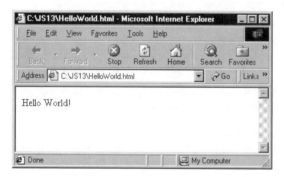

Figure 1.11 *Our script as it appears in the browser*

1.3.2   Comments

We now come to a few issues that don't have much to do with programming in JavaScript, but are very important for making programs easier to understand: comments. There are several different ways to insert comments in JavaScript. One way is to use //, to tell the browser that a comment is about to follow. // ensures that everything contained in the line following // will be evaluated by the browser as a comment. Sometimes you may want to add more than just a short comment, for example if you wanted to describe a function or another part of the program in detail over several lines. You might want to explain how the function or source text works and what sort of entry values are expected. In this case, the browsers allow us to simplify the comments. The /* string tells the browser that all of the following lines in the source text are to be treated as comment and do not need to be translated. To prevent the whole source code from being handled as comment after we have entered /*, we also need a string to tell the browser that the comment is finished and that it should translate everything again starting from this point. The string for ending the comment is */. The program is translated again after this string.

1.3.3   Browsers that do not have JavaScript capability

Because JavaScript has developed very quickly as a language, many browsers do not yet support all standards, so your programs may not necessarily run on these browsers. To prevent a browser from executing uncontrolled actions on a JavaScript that it cannot translate, there are ways to check which JavaScript version a user's browser supports before starting the program. This issue will be covered later on, so for the moment we would simply point out that the way to make these checks or restrictions is explained in section 1.7. You already know one way to determine which version of JavaScript is used to translate a program: by specifying the LANGUAGE="JavaScript" attribute in the <SCRIPT> tag in HTML. You can also assign the LANGUAGE attribute one of the following values:

→ JavaScript1.1
→ JavaScript1.2
→ JavaScript1.3

For example, a browser that only supports JavaScript version 1.1 will ignore a script written for JavaScript1.3.

1.4   Variables

This section will show how you can work with variables under JavaScript and how to write easily readable source code. We will also deal briefly with the conventions for JavaScript syntax.

1.4.1   What is the point of variables?

Variables are needed to save values you will want to use at a later stage. Because the value of a variable doesn't tell you very much, we usually assign variable names that provide an intuitive link indicating the type of value stored in these variables.

Another advantage of well-chosen variable names is the fact that the source text can be made more meaningful. For example, the following source code doesn't tell you much about the calculations involved:

```
var noIdea
var whoKnows
noIdea = (whoKnows / 100) *17.5
```

Meaningful variable names would help you to see at a glance exactly what is being calculated, even after several years. Here are some examples of meaningful variable names:

```
var vatItem
var itemPrice
vatItem = (itemPrice / 100) * 17.5
```

The choice of these variable names means that the person reading the source code will immediately know what kind of calculation is being made.

It is up to you whether you write your source code in a way that can be easily read by others or whether you prefer a more cryptic approach. All we can say at this point is that you will make life easier for yourself if you choose meaningful variable names. You will also make it easier to work in a team with other programmers.

1.4.2   Declaring and initializing variables

There are two ways to declare a variable in JavaScript. You can simply assign a value to the variable:

```
x = 10
```

or use the keyword var to indicate that a variable is now being declared:

```
var x = 10
```

The result of both declaration methods is the same: Variable x is assigned the value 10.

To save space when defining variables and to define several variables in succession, you can use the following syntax:

```
x = 10; y = 20;
```

```
var x = 10; var y = 20;
```

This notation uses ; to separate commands from one another.

The following syntax can also be used:

```
var x = 10, y = 20
```

However, you can only use this syntax in association with the keyword var.

A JavaScript can contain more than just integer type variables. For example, to initialize an array you need the following syntax:

```
new myArray(10)
```

This command creates an array called myArray containing 10 elements that as yet have no values. The following syntax is used to assign values to the various elements in the array:

```
myArray[0] = "Value1"
myArray[9] = "Value10"
```

These assignments set the value of the first array element (myArray[0]) to "Value1" and the value of the last array element (myArray[9]) to "Value10".

Finally, to define a string, proceed as follows:

```
var name = new String("Miller")
```

The statement defines the variable name as a string object and assigns it the value "Miller".

1.4.3   Naming conventions

The table below lists the reserved words in JavaScript 1.3 that cannot be used for variable, method, function or object names. All words listed here are used as keywords in the versions of JavaScript published to date or are already reserved for later versions.

Reserved words			
abstract	else	instanceof	switch
boolean	enum	int	synchronized
break	export	interface	this
byte	extends	long	throw
case	false	native	throws
catch	final	new	transient
char	finally	null	true
class	float	package	try
const	for	private	typeof

Reserved words			
continue	function	protected	var
debugger	goto	public	void
default	if	return	volatile
delete	implements	short	while
do	import	static	with
double	in	super	

Table 1.3   *Reserved words in JavaScript 1.3*

Strings also contain reserved control characters that can be used to format the text or to insert special characters like quotes into a string.

Table 1.4 contains a list of special characters in strings.

Character	Meaning
\b	Backspace
\f	Form feed
\n	New line
\r	Carriage return
\t	Tab
\'	Apostrophe (')
\"	Quotation marks (")
\\	Backslash (\ )
\XXX	A character from the Latin-1 character set that is specified more precisely by up to three octal numbers. Range from 0 to 377, where \251 stands for the copyright symbol, for example.
\xXX	Hexadecimal value
\uXXXX	Unicode characters

Table 1.4   *Special characters in strings*

It is important that all special characters should start with a \ as otherwise they would be handled as normal text rather than as control characters.

JavaScript is case-sensitive in names for commands, variables, objects, etc. while HTML permits some freedom.

1.4.4   Data types and literals

The following data types are known in JavaScript:

→ Numbers
→ Boolean values
→ Strings

There are two different versions of all of these data types: single values and objects. At this point we will concentrate on the values. Section 1.7 will deal with the objects in more detail.

In the case of numbers, no explicit distinction is made between integer values and decimal numbers. You do not need special notation to use whole numbers in your programs, so you can use the familiar decimal format. However, you can also use an alternative octal or hexadecimal format for numbers. To use these alternatives, you must follow a special syntax when writing numbers. For octal numbers this is indicated by a prefixed 0 (zero). An 0x (or 0X) prefix is used for hexadecimal numbers. Of course, octal numbers only allow you to enter numbers in the range 0 to 7, while the decimal system allows numbers 0 to 9. Things are very different in the hexadecimal system; here numbers from 0 to 9 are permitted and letters from A to F (or a to f).

Decimal	Octal (prefix 0)	Hexadecimal (prefix 0x)
0	00	0x0
1	01	0x1
2	02	0x2
4	04	0x4
8	010	0x8
10	012	0xA
15	017	0xF
16	020	0x10
20	024	0x14
24	030	0x18
255	0377	0xFF

Table 1.5   *Examples of decimal, octal and hexadecimal notation*

The appendix contains a complete conversion table for all numbers from 0 to 255.

Things are different for numbers containing decimal points. There are two different notations to choose from.

Fixed point notation	Floating point notation	Mathematical notation
1.0	1e0	$1*10^0$
	.1e1	$0.1*10^1$
0.0000002	2e-7	$2*10^{-7}$
	.2e-6	$0.2*10^{-6}$
-272120000000000	-2.7212e14	$-2.7212*10^{14}$
-0.00012	-.12e-3	$-0.12*10^{-3}$

Table 1.6 *Real numbers in fixed and floating point notation*

Things get easier when you use strings and Boolean expressions. With these data types all you need to do is create a variable and assign it the value you want. So, the following syntax is enough to create a string:

```
var Text = "This variable contains text."
```

or, for a Boolean expression:

```
var YesNo = true
```

However, we should point out here that you can only perform string operations with string objects. You will learn more about how to create and use objects in the relevant section below.

1.4.5   Operators

JavaScript has assignment, compare, arithmetic, bitwise, logical, string and special operators. One important thing about operators is the syntax. For example, let's look at the increment operator (++). To increment a value before assigning it, you use ++x (prefix); to increment the value after assignment, you write x++ (postfix). Let's take a look at an example:

```
var a, b, pref, postf;
pre = 10;
post = 10;
a=++pref;
b=postf++;
```

pref and postf have value 10 to begin with. a=++pref; just means: first increment pref by 1 and assign the result to a. a and pref therefore both have value 11 after the statement. b=postf++; could therefore be translated as: assign to b the value of postf and increment postf by 1. Therefore the value of b after this statement is 10 and postf has the value 11.

The following tables provide an overview of the operators.

Operator	Description
+	(Addition) adds two numbers together.
++	(Increment) increases the value of a variable by one.
-	(Subtraction) subtracts one number from another.
- -	(Decrement) decreases the value of a variable by one.
*	(Multiplication) multiplies two numbers together.
/	(Division) divides one number by another.
%	(Modulo) outputs the whole number remainder when one number is divided by another.

Table 1.7 *Arithmetic operators*

Operator	Description
+	(String addition) links two strings together.
+=	Concatenates the string on right of the operator to the variable on the left.

Table 1.8 *String operators*

Operator	Description
&&	(Logical AND) returns the value `true` if both operands have the value `true`.
||	(Logical OR) returns the value `true` if one of the operands has the value `true`.
!	(Logical NOT) negates the operand.

Table 1.9 *Logical operators*

Operator	Description
&	Bitwise AND.
^	Bitwise XOR.
|	Bitwise OR.
~	Bitwise NOT.
<<	Shift left.
>>	Shift right.
>>>	Shift right with zero padding.

Table 1.10 *Bitwise operators*

Operator	Description
=	Assigns the value of the second operand to the first operand.

Operator	Description
+=	Adds two numbers together and saves the result in the first number.
-=	Subtracts one number from another and saves the result in the first number.
*=	Multiplies two numbers and saves the result in the first number.
/=	Divides one number by another and assigns the result to the first number.
%=	Calculates the modulo of two operands and assigns the result to the first operand.
&=	Performs a bitwise AND link and saves the result in the first operand.
^=	Performs a bitwise XOR link and saves the result in the first operand.
|=	Performs a bitwise OR link and saves the result in the first operand.
<<=	Bitwise assignment with left shift.
>>=	Bitwise assignment with right shift.
>>>=	Bitwise assignment with right shift with zero padding.

Table 1.11 *Assignment operators*

Operator	Description
==	Returns the value true if both operands are equal.
!=	Returns the value true if both operands are not equal.
===	Returns the value true if both operands are equal and have the same data type.
!==	Returns the value true if both operands are not equal and/or both operands have the same data type.
>	Returns the value true if the left operand is greater than the right operand.
>=	Returns the value true if the left operand is greater than or equal to the right operand.
<	Returns the value true if the left operand is less than the right one.
<=	Returns the value true if the left operand is less than or equal to the right operand.

Table 1.12 *Compare operators*

Operator	Description
?:	Simplified notation for an "if...then...else" inquiry.
,	The commas are used to keep elements separate.
delete	Deletes an object, a property of an object or an element in an array.
new	Creates an instance of a user-defined object or predefined object.

Operator	Description
this	Keyword you can use to refer to the current object.
typeof	Returns a string containing the type of the unevaluated operand.
void	Defined return for functions that do not return a value.

Table 1.13 *Special operator*

Operator hierarchy:

Name	Operator / Operators
Comma	,
Assignment	= += -= *= /= %= <<= >>= >>>= &= ^= |=
Condition	? :
Logical OR	||
Logical AND	&&
Bitwise OR	|
Bitwise XOR	^
Bitwise AND	&
Equals	== !=
Compare	< <= > >=
Bitwise shift	<< >> >>>
Addition / subtraction	+ -
Multiplication / division	* / %
Inversion/ increment	! ~ - + ++ -- typeof void delete
Call	( )
Originating instance	new
Member	. [ ]

Table 1.14 *Operator precedence from highest (first row) to lowest*

1.4.6 JavaScript entities

It sometimes happens that the variables defined in JavaScript are also needed in the HTML part of a page. This is where the JavaScript entities of Netscape Navigator are used. That's right. The JavaScript entities are only supported by Netscape and not by Microsoft. To be able to use a variable defined in the <SCRIPT> part of the page, the variable must addressed as follows &{variable};. In our example, the width variable described in the <SCRIPT> tag is transferred to an input field.

```
<HTML>
  <HEAD>
    <SCRIPT LANGUAGE="JavaScript">
    var width = 10;
    </SCRIPT>
  </HEAD>
  <BODY>
  <FORM>
    <INPUT TYPE="TEXT" SIZE=&{width};>
  </FORM>
  </BODY>
</HTML>
```

The browser display should look like this:

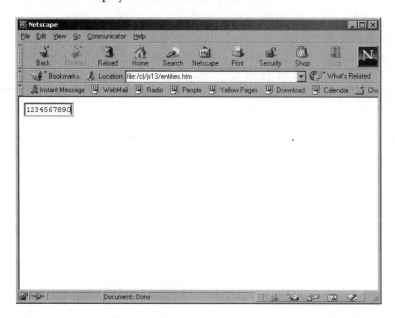

Figure 1.12 *A text field that takes its width from a JavaScript variable*

Don't worry that your text field contains no numbers. We only entered these to show that the field really is 10 characters wide.

JavaScript entities are very useful when you are writing a page for Netscape browser only. Otherwise you should try to manage without them for the sake of compatibility.

This section explains how to declare and then call functions. When you have completed this part, you will have no problem using your own functions and functions provided by other programmers or making your functions available to other programmers.

1.5.1 What is the point of functions?

Functions perform one of the key tasks in JavaScript. They allow you to develop frequently recurring problems just once and then to call them up again and again as and when they are needed. This makes life much easier because you can pass variables when you call functions and can then assign the results of the function to a variable.

1.5.2 Transfer values

Values that are to be transferred to a function must always be transferred in brackets when the function is called. Here's an example of a function with transfer parameters:

```
myFunction(firstVariable, secondVariable)
```

Two variables were transferred in this example.

If you wanted to implement a function without transferring parameters, the function call would look like this:

```
myFunction()
```

We can only see whether the variables transferred to a function still keep the same original names in the function by looking at the definition of the function itself. By the way, you can also transfer fixed values, such as a `string` or numbers to a function. In other words, you don't have to place the value or values you want to transfer in variables, but can instead transfer them directly. The next example contains a complete definition of a function in which two variables are transferred and then called:

```
function myFunction(number, text) {
  for (var counter = 0; counter < number; counter++) {
    alert(text);
  }
}
var Message = "Hello!";
myFunction(3, message);
```

This example would open an information dialog containing the text `Hello!` three times in succession. If you take a closer look at the source code, you will see that the names `number` and `text` were chosen for the variable transfer in the definition. So in our example the `number` variable with have the value 3 and the `text` variable would have the value `Hello!`. But, you may well ask, what about the `message` variable? Do you have to create the variable? Don't worry, with small programs like this we could have done without the variable and transferred the text of the message as a fixed value. We just wanted to show you how to program a parameter transfer with variables. You can also get values back from a function. In other words you can receive values from the function rather than transferring them to the function. These are called `return` values.

1.5.3   Local and global variables

The following example creates a variable named `number` and assigns it the value `10` on a global basis. After that `number` is transferred to the `myFunction()` function. The function handles the value transferred internally as a separate variable. It doesn't matter if the variable has the same name as a variable defined outside of the function (global variable), as in our example. The global variable is not altered by our function, but only the internal (local) variable with the same name. Key in the following code and save the file as `localglobal.htm`.

```
<HTML>
  <HEAD>
    <SCRIPT LANGUAGE="JavaScript">
      Function myFunction(number) {
        document.write("Number in function: "+number);
        number += 2;
        document.write("Number in function: "+number);
      }

    var number = 10;
    document.write("Number directly following initializa-
tion: "+number);
    myFunction(number);
```

```
        document.write("Number after return from function:
                "+number);
    </SCRIPT>
  </HEAD>
</HTML>
```

The following should appear in the browser window when the function is called:

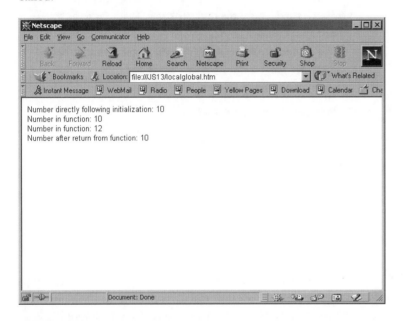

Figure 1.13 *The difference between a local and global variable*

1.5.4   Predefined functions

The following table contains a list of the predefined functions available in Java-Script.

Function	Description
escape()	Returns the hexadecimal coding for a string transferred in ISO-Latin-1
eval()	Calculates the transferred string and returns the result
isFinite()	Checks that a transferred number is a valid number
isNaN()	Checks whether or not the transferred value is a number. This method returns the value true if the tested value is not a number.
Number()	Converts the transferred object into a number

Function	Description
parse- Float()	Transforms a string into a floating point number.
parseInt()	Transforms a string into an integer.
String()	Converts the object transferred into a string.
taint()	Encrypts data elements or scripts.
unescape()	Converts all characters in the transferred string into normal ASCII characters and returns the resulting string. The string to be transferred must contain a percentage sign (%) and the hexadecimal value of the character from the ASCII character table for each character to be converted.
untaint()	Decrypts data elements or scripts.

Table 1.15 *Predefined functions of JavaScript*

Tip See Section 2.2 for more details about the different functions.

1.6 Loops and jumps

Next we want to show you how to manage the loops and jumps you can make in JavaScript 1.3. This section will use practical examples to show the differences between the various loops and when to use which loop.

1.6.1 if...else

The if query is the most frequently used query in all programming languages. You can use the if query to perform a simple comparison between two values or states. If we didn't have this query, our programs would have to stick rigidly to one single route through the program and could not react to different variable states with different programming code. The following chart shows the program flow of an if query.

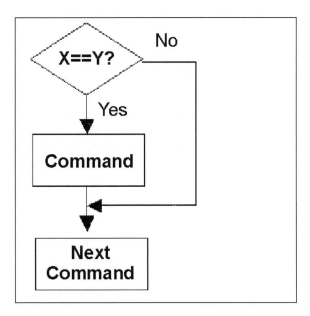

Figure 1.14 *Flowchart for an* `if` *query*

Example:

```
if (x > y) document.write("x is greater than y");
```

In this example, a check is made to see whether variable x is greater than variable y. If this is the case (in other words, the condition returns the value `true`), then `document.write("x is greater than y");` is executed. If x is not greater than y, then the `document.write("x is greater than y");` statement is simply skipped and the next command in the program is executed.

If you want to execute more than one command after checking whether x is greater than y, you should enter all statements in parentheses following the `if` query.

```
if (x > y) {
  document.write("x is greater than y");
  document.write("<BR>  The value of x: " + x);
  document.write("<BR>  The value of y: " + y);
}
```

If x is greater than y this time, then all commands in parentheses are executed. If x is not greater than y, then all statements in parentheses are skipped.

We can also use the `if` query to make allowance for the fact that the condition of the `if` query may not be met. This is where the `else` command is used, as shown below.

```
if (x > y) {
  document.write("x is greater than y");
  document.write("<BR>  The value of x: " + x);
  document.write("<BR>  The value of y: " + y);
} else document.write("x is not greater than y");
```

If the `if` query is not met here, then the statement following the `else` is executed. You can also use `else` to execute several commands at once. Just place the commands in parentheses as shown above and they will be executed. Figure 1.15 shows the flow for an `if...else` query.

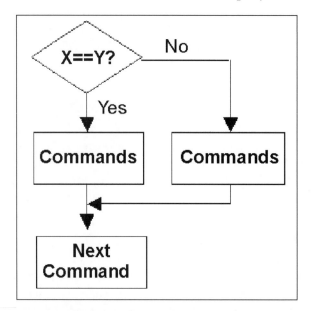

Figure 1.15 *The* `if...else` *query*

You can also create nested `if` queries. What does nested mean? In this case it just means that an `if` query contained in one of the result branches (in other words directly following the `if` or the `else`) executes a second `if` query.

```
if (x == y) {
  if (y == z) {
    document.write("x is equal to y and equal to z");
  }
}
```

In this case a check is made as soon as x is equal to y to see whether y is also equal to z. The `document.write("x is equal to y and equal to z");` command is only executed when both `if` queries are met. If just one of the two if queries in this example was not met, then the next command in the program would be called up and the whole branch of if queries would be skipped.

There is a shorthand version of the if query:

```
(x > y) ? document.write("x is greater than y") : docu-
ment.write("x is not greater than y");
```

does just the same job as:

```
if (x > y) {
  document.write("x is greater than y");
} else document.write("x is not greater than y");
```

However, you can do more with this notation than just shorten the if query. You can also use ?: to implement the following code:

```
possible = (x > y) ? "yes" : "no";
```

1.6.2   switch

If you want to evaluate several options in a single query, then the switch query is just what you're looking for. A switch query actually contains several if queries that are executed one after the other. As soon as one of the query parameters matches the value required, the switch query jumps to the right branch for this case and executes the program code contained there. You can also use the switch statement to build in a branch that is executed if none of the above conditions is met. Let's take a look at the switch statement in program code.

```
switch (valueToBeChecked) {
  case 1 :
    document.write("A 1 has been transferred.<BR>");
    break;
  case "2" :
    document.write("A 2 has been transferred.<BR>");
    break;
  case 3 :
    document.write("A 3 has been transferred.<BR>");
    break;
default :
    document.write("Neither 1, '2' nor 3 has been trans-
ferred.<BR>");
    break;
}
```

In this example, the value transferred to the switch query in the valueToBe-Checked variable is checked. It is important to note what you are checking for in the `case` sections. JavaScript differentiates between a number, letter or string in this case. In the last example, the `case "2" :` statement does not react to the number 2, but rather to the string 2.

1.6.3   for

The `for` loop is a repeat loop which you can use to repeat statements as often as you want. This loop is particularly useful when you come across problems in which parts of a program need to be executed several times in succession. In the next example, a variable is incremented by one ten times and displayed.

```
<HTML>
  <HEAD>
    <SCRIPT LANGUAGE="JavaScript">
      for (var i = 0; i < 10; i++) {
        document.write("i == "+i+"<BR>");
      }
    </SCRIPT>
  </HEAD>
</HTML>
```

After this program is complete, the browser should look like Figure 1.16.

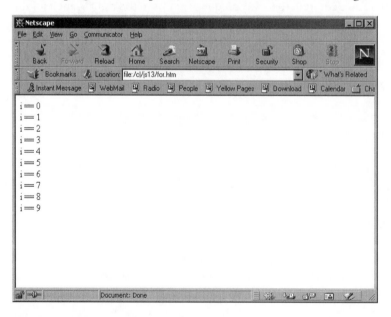

Figure 1.16 *Output for a* `for` *loop*

Figure 1.17 shows the program flow of the `for` loop.

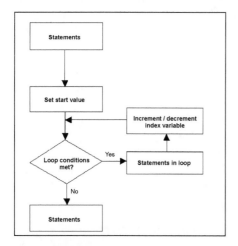

Figure 1.17 *The* `for` *loop*

1.6.4 while

The `while` loop is very similar to the `for` loop execpt that the `while` loop only executes whilst a particular condition is met. When the condition test fails the loop terminates and execution continues with the next line in your program. `While` loops do not intialize or update the variables that you may be testing, you must do this yourself. The flowchart for a `while` loop shows this clearly (Figure 1.18).

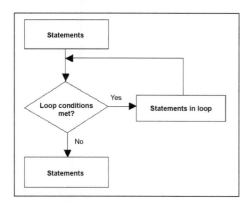

Figure 1.18 *The* `while` *loop*

If we wanted to use the `while` loop instead of the `for` loop in our example, then the source text would have to look like this:

```
<HTML>
  <HEAD>
    <SCRIPT LANGUAGE="JavaScript">
      var i = 0;
      while (i < 10) {
        document.write("i == "+i+"<BR>");
        i++;
      }
    </SCRIPT>
  </HEAD>
</HTML>
```

The `while` loop looks the same as the `for` loop in the browser.

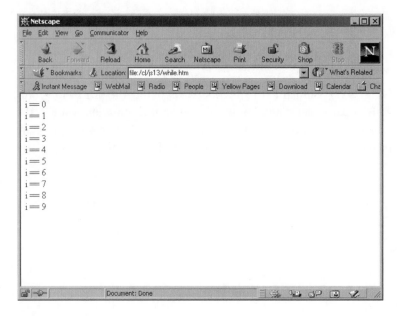

Figure 1.19 *The* `while` *loop*

The `while` loop is useful when you want to execute a piece of code a number of times until a particular condition is true, without having to predetermine the number of iterations.

1.6.5   break

This terminates the current branch of a loop or query and executes the next command following the terminated branch.

1.6.6   continue

This terminates the current loop or query and executes the next command following the loop or query.

1.6.7   do...while

This executes the statements specified in the loop until the query condition becomes `false`. This is different from the normal `while` loop because the statements in the `do...while` loop are executed at least once, regardless of whether the condition in the loop is met or not.

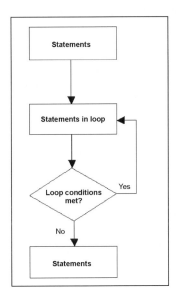

Figure 1.20   *The* `do...while` *loop*

Let's go back again to the example of the `for` loop and rewrite the program for the `do...while` loop.

```
<HTML>
  <HEAD>
    <SCRIPT LANGUAGE="JavaScript">
      var i = 0;
      do {
```

```
          document.write("i == "+i+"<BR>");
          i++;
        } while (i < 10);
      </SCRIPT>
    </HEAD>
</HTML>
```

As expected, the result looks exactly the same as in the two previous loops. But if we change variable i before the loop runs for the first time, so that it contains the value 20, the for and while loops would not display anything in the browser.

```
<HTML>
  <HEAD>
    <SCRIPT LANGUAGE="JavaScript">
      var i = 20;
      do {
        document.write("i == "+i+"<BR>");
        i++;
      } while (i < 10);
    </SCRIPT>
  </HEAD>
</HTML>
```

Things are different with a do...while loop (Figure 1.21).

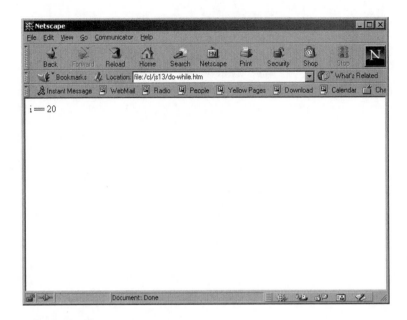

Figure 1.21 *Result of a* do...while *loop*

Even though the termination condition was met, the do...while loop still ran once.

1.6.8   for...in

This executes a for loop with an object. This is very helpful if you don't know exactly how many elements an object contains. Because you should know how to create and use objects for this loop, please check Section 1.7.6 for a detailed description of this type of loop.

1.6.9   Recursive functions

Recursive functions are functions that call themselves. No doubt you're wondering: what's the point of that? Admittedly most programs can be created using perfectly ordinary functions. But in some exceptional cases it is easier to program a function recursively. The best-known example of a recursive function is the calculation of a factorial. From a mathematical viewpoint, factorial 7 is simply the result of the calculation 7*6*5*4*3*2*1 or, in mathematical notation, 7!. A program for this problem might look like this:

```
<HTML>
  <HEAD>
    <SCRIPT LANGUAGE="JavaScript">
```

```
      function factorial(value) {
        if (value != 1) {
          return value * factorial(value-1);
        }
        else {
          return 1;
        }
      }
      function whatNumber() {
        var number;
        number = prompt("Please enter a number:", "");
        alert("The factorial of " + number + " is " + facto-
rial(number) + ".");
      }
      </SCRIPT>
    </HEAD>
    <BODY>
    <FORM>
      <INPUT TYPE="BUTTON" VALUE="Factorial of ..."
             onclick="whatNumber()">
    </FORM>
    </BODY>
</HTML>
```

The majority of the programs will not need to use a recursive function. You can normally acheive the same result with a normal loop.

1.7   Objects

Objects are important components of JavaScript. This section is designed to illustrate selected objects and how these are used in JavaScript, so that you will be able to use all available objects without difficulty.

1.7.1   What is the purpose of objects?

Objects are used in programming languages to store data in a structured way. For example, if you reduce a car to data that could be understood by the computer, you could create an object called car that has several properties and methods. The properties represent values that describe your car in greater detail, i.e. engine statistics or the number of wheels your car has. The methods are functions that belong to the object and that allow you to request or alter data about the object. For example, set and get methods are very popular as these output the properties of the object in formatted form or save them in the object. However, because our aim in this section is firstly to deal with existing objects in JavaScript and not to define our own objects immediately, let's start by introducing the objects that have already been implemented in JavaScript.

1.7.2 Defining objects

The predefined objects in JavaScript exist as definitions and, in most cases, you cannot use them directly. To allow us to use these objects we must make instances of the objects. An instance is just the conversion of the defined object (which you cannot yet use) into a real object you can work with. When you create an instance, you assign a name to the object that you can use to address it later. You create an instance of an object using its constructor in the computer's memory. In most cases, an object's constructor is introduced with the keyword new. A constructor is the method of the object that is responsible for creating an instance of an object. The section on self-defined objects will take a closer look at the constructor method. We don't need to create instances for the following JavaScript objects because they are created automatically by the JavaScript engine:

→ window
→ document
→ location
→ history
→ navigator

1.7.3 Properties and methods

To access properties or methods of an object you must know the name of the object and property or method you want to call up. For example, you would assign the cc property of the object car to the variable x with the following syntax.

```
x = car.cc
```

To assign a value to the cc property, just reverse the syntax.

```
car.cc = "1.6 litres"
```

To call up a function of the object car that displays all of the object's properties – which would be called allData – you use the following syntax.

```
car.allData()
```

There's another shortcut for assigning properties. If you want to assign values to several properties of the same object in succession, you can use the with statement to make your work shorter.

```
with (car) {
```

```
name = "Vectra"
manufacturer = "Vauxhall"
cc = "1.6 litres"
color = "Blue"
}
```

This with statement is the simplified notation for:

```
car.name = "Vectra"
car.manufacturer = "Vauxhall"
car.cc = "1.6 litres"
car.color = "Blue"
```

This might not seem to make things a lot simpler in our example, but you will find with very useful when objects have long names.

1.7.4 Objects on the Internet page

The following objects are created automatically by the JavaScript engine and do not need to be created using a constructor.

The window object represents the browser window. Methods like open(), close(), alert(), confirm() and prompt() are defined in the window object and enable you to open and close windows quickly and easily and to obtain information from users. The following program opens a window using the window object.

```
<HTML>
  <HEAD>
    <SCRIPT LANGUAGE="JavaScript">
    var myWindow;

    function openNewWindow() {
      myWindow = open("http://www.aw.com/cseng/");
    }
    </SCRIPT>
  </HEAD>
  <BODY>
    <FORM>
      <INPUT TYPE="BUTTON" VALUE="Addison-Wesley"
                  onclick="openNewWindow()">
    </FORM>
  </BODY>
</HTML>
```

You're sure to have noticed that we called the `open()` method of the `window` object with `open()`, instead of `window.open()`. This is because the `window` object is a special object and methods of the `window` object can be called without specifying `window`. However, this only works for the `window` object and not for other objects. To close the open window, we simply modify the program.

```html
<HTML>
  <HEAD>
    <SCRIPT LANGUAGE="JavaScript">
    var myWindow;

    function openNewWindow() {
      myWindow = open("http://www.aw.com/cseng/");
    }
    function closeNewWindow() {
      myWindow.close();
    }
    </SCRIPT>
  </HEAD>
  <BODY>
    <FORM>
      <INPUT TYPE="BUTTON" VALUE="Addison-Wesley"
             onclick="openNewWindow()">
      <INPUT TYPE="BUTTON" VALUE="close"
             onclick="closeNewWindow()">
    </FORM>
  </BODY>
</HTML>
```

It is very important to specify the object name of the `window` object you want to close when using the `close()` method. If you try to close a window that was not created using JavaScript, then the user will see a popup window asking whether the window can be closed.

To open a window with a particular appearance, you can include more details of how the window should look in the `open()` method.

```html
<HTML>
  <HEAD>
    <SCRIPT LANGUAGE="JavaScript">
    var myWindow;

    function openNewWindow() {
      myWindow = open("http://www.aw.com/cseng/",
                 "AddisonWesleyWin-
```

```
dow","height=300,width=800");
    }
    </SCRIPT>
  </HEAD>
  <BODY>
    <FORM>
      <INPUT TYPE="BUTTON" VALUE="Addison-Wesley"
            onclick="openNewWindow()">
    </FORM>
  </BODY>
</HTML>
```

The program should then open the window shown in Figure 1.22.

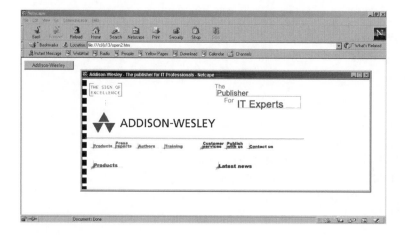

Figure 1.22 *An adapted window*

The "AddisonWesleyWindow" string stands for the name of the window that is used to access the window from other JavaScript programs or HTML pages.

Next let's take another look at the alert(), confirm() and prompt() methods.

alert() returns a dialog box which the user can close by clicking on the relevant OK button. A message transferred by a string is displayed within the dialog. You will already be familiar with a one-line output in a dialog field with alert() from the previous chapters. But you can also transfer messages covering several lines to the alert() method.

```
alert("This text\nshould cover\nseveral lines.")
```

Here \n forces a line break.

Figure 1.23 *Displaying messages covering several lines*

The `confirm()` method allows the user to react to a message with an OK or Cancel button. The result of the `confirm()` method is a Boolean expression that is `true` when you click OK and `false` when you click Cancel. You can assign the result directly to a variable.

```
YesNo = confirm("Are you really sure?");
```

Figure 1.24 *Using the* `confirm()` *method*

Finally, there is the `prompt()` method which allows you to obtain input from the user.

```
input = prompt("Your guess for a number between 0 and 100?",
"Please enter your guess here.")
```

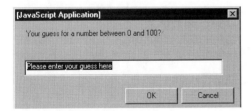

Figure 1.25 *User input with* `prompt()`

After you press OK, the value you have entered is transferred to the `input` variable. However, if you cancel this dialog by pressing `Cancel` then the `false` value is returned.

The `navigator` object represents the browser. Properties such as `appCode-Name`, `appName`, `appVersion`, `platform` and `userAgent` are defined in the `navigator`. You can use these to get information about the user's browser quickly and easily. The following program displays information about your browser.

```
<HTML>
  <HEAD>
    <SCRIPT LANGUAGE="JavaScript">
    with (document) {
      write("appCodeName: "+navigator.appCodeName+"<BR>");
      write("appName: "+navigator.appName+"<BR>");
      write("appVersion: "+navigator.appVersion+"<BR>");
      write("platform: "+navigator.platform+"<BR>");
      write("userAgent: "+navigator.userAgent+"<BR>");
    }
    </SCRIPT>
  </HEAD>
</HTML>
```

If you are using a Netscape browser your display will look something like Figure 1.26.

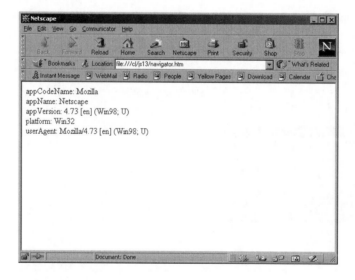

Figure 1.26 *Contents of the navigator object with a Netscape browser*

If you are using Microsoft Internet Explorer then the display will look like Figure 1.27.

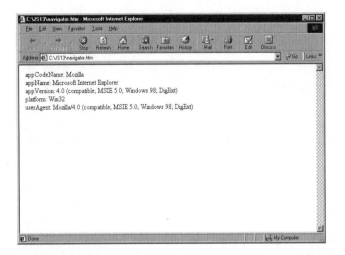

Figure 1.27 *Contents of the navigator object with a Microsoft browser*

It should by easy enough to check if a user is using the browser required for your script. For example, if you have a page optimized for Netscape Navigator and want to check if the user is also using this browser, you could react to incorrect browsers with the following program and draw the user's attention to optimized compatibility with the other browser.

```
if (navigator.appName.indexOf("Netscape") != -1) {
  document.write("You are using Netscape
             Communicator/Navigator.");
} else {
  document.write("You are not using Netscape
             Communicator/Navigator.");
}
```

You could also use the same program for Microsoft Internet Explorer.

```
if (navigator.appName.indexOf("Microsoft Internet Explorer
") != -1) {
  document.write("You are using Microsoft Internet
Explorer.");
} else {
  document.write("You are not using Microsoft Internet
Explorer.");
}
```

You can use the indexOf method to check if a string contains a specified character sequence. It should therefore be easy to check for all possible versions of browsers regardless of the names or version numbers.

1.7.5   Predefined objects

The quick reference guide contains a list of all objects available in JavaScript.

1.7.6   User-defined objects

As promised at the start of this section, we now come to the definition of our own objects. The first thing we need – naturally enough – is an object we want to implement. Let's take an object that describes a person and stores the following properties for this person:

→ surname
→ first name
→ age

To implement these properties for our object, we need a program that contains the constructor for our object.

```
function person(surname, first name, age) {
// The elements of the object.
this.surname = surname;
this.first name = first name;
this.age = age;
}
```

As you can see, the constructor of the object is just a normal function which is assigned values and which then assigns these values to an object. Once we have created the constructor for our object, we can create instances of the object.

```
person1 = new person("Delwood", "John", "26");
```

Here's a complete program that you could use to file information on several people:

```
<HTML>
  <SCRIPT>
    function person(surname, first_name, age) {
      // The elements of the object.
      this.surname = surname;
      this.first_name = first_name;
      this.age = age;
    }
    // Create the first instance.
    person1 = new person("Delwood", "John", "26");
    // Create the second instance.
    person2 = new person("Delwood", "Edward", "25");
    with (document) {
```

```
        // Display the first instance.
        write(person1.first_name + " " + person1.surname + "
is "
            + person1.age + " years old.<BR>");
        // Display the second instance.
        write(person2.first_name + " " + person2.surname + "
is "
            + person2.age + " years old.<BR>");
    }
  </SCRIPT>
</HTML>
```

If you don't want to program the name display every time with docu-
ment.write() but would prefer to call up a method to perform this task, then
you would have to expand our object as follows:

```
function person(surname, first name, age) {
// The elements of the object.
this.surname = surname;
this.first_name = first_name;
this.age = age;

// The methods of the object.
this.output = output;
}
```

Note that the statement this.output = output; has no brackets after output, as otherwise the output function would be called immediately, which is
not what we want. The complete program for our object now looks like this:

```
<HTML>
  <SCRIPT>
    function person(surname, first name, age) {
      // The elements of the object.
      this.surname = surname;
      this.first name = first name;
      this.age = age;

      // The methods of the object.
      this.output = output;
    }
    function output() {
      with (document) {
        write(this.first name + " " + this.surname + " is "
+ this.age + "
```

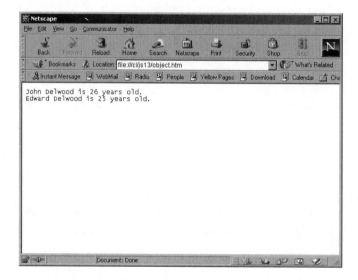
```
                    years old.<BR>");
    }
  }
  // Create the instances.
  person1 = new person("Delwood", "John", "26");
  person2 = new person("Delwood", "Edward", "25");

  //Call method.
  person1.output();
  person2.output();
</SCRIPT>
</HTML>
```

Figure 1.28 shows the program output.

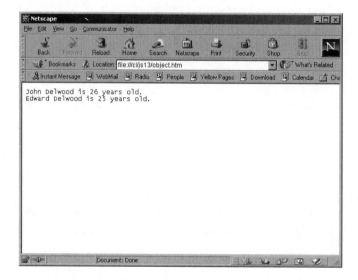

Figure 1.28 *User-defined objects with a separate* output() *method*

The this variable refers to the object on which you are operating. In our example, the person function creates a new object by updating the attributes of the this variable. The this variable is the variable which is returned as an object to the caller.

Finally, we should mention the function of the for...in loop. All this loop does is to run through all the attributes in an object. Example:

```
<HTML>
  <SCRIPT>
    function person(surname, first name, age) {
      // The elements of the object.
      this.surname = surname;
      this.first name = first name;
      this.age = age;
    }
// Create the instances.
    person1 = new person("Delwood", "John", "26");

    for (i in person1) {
      document.write( i + ": ");
      document.write( person1[i] + "<BR>");
    }
  </SCRIPT>
</HTML>
```

This for...in loop creates the output shown in Figure 1.29.

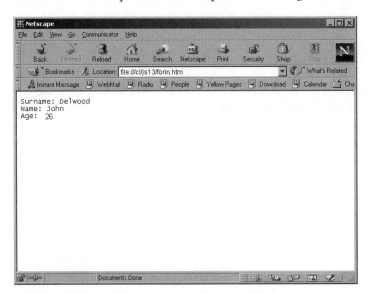

Figure 1.29 *Output of the* for...in *loop*

This type of loop is very useful when working with arrays.

1.8 Events

This section introduces events and their handlers. We're going to show you how to check for particular events and to follow these up with actions.

1.8.1   What is the purpose of events?

Event handlers allow you to react to events triggered by an HTML element. When you are programming the HTML element, the syntax for event handlers involves assigning an event handler to the attribute and specifying what is to happen in this event.

```
<FORM>
    <INPUT TYPE=BUTTON VALUE="Please press!"
onClick="alert('Button has been pressed!')">
</FORM>
```

This example would return the message window shown in Figure 1.30 if you pressed the button created on the HTML page.

Figure 1.30   *The result of our event handler*

You can also specify function names instead of the JavaScript code, allowing you to react to events with complex programs.

1.8.2   Event handler

Table 1.16 contains a list of the event handlers available in JavaScript.

Event	Event handler	Description
Abort	onAbort	Executes a JavaScript code if the user cancels an action.
Blur	onBlur	Executes a JavaScript code if an element of a form, window or frame loses focus.
Change	onChange	Executes a JavaScript code if a select, text or text area input field loses focus and if its data has been changed.
Click	onClick	Executes a JavaScript code if an element is clicked in a form.

Event	Event handler	Description
DblClick	onDblClick	Executes a JavaScript code if an element is double-clicked in a form.
DragDrop	onDragDrop	Executes a JavaScript code if the user drags an object (file, etc.) into the browser window and drops it there.
Error	onError	Executes a JavaScript code if an error occurs while loading a document or image.
Focus	onFocus	Executes a JavaScript when an element comes into focus.
KeyDown	onKeyDown	Executes a JavaScript code when a key on the keyboard is pressed down.
KeyPress	onKeyPress	Executes a JavaScript code when the user presses a key or holds a key down.
KeyUp	onKeyUp	Executes a JavaScript code when a key on the keyboard is released again.
Load	onLoad	Executes a JavaScript code when the browser has finished loading a document or all the frames in a FRAMESET tag.
Mouse-Down	onMouseDown	Executes a JavaScript code when the user presses down a mouse key.
Mouse-Move	onMouseMove	Executes a JavaScript code when the user moves the mouse.
MouseOut	onMouseOut	Executes a JavaScript code when the mouse pointer moves out of an area (image or link). The mouse pointer must have been inside the area prior to this.
Mouse-Over	onMouseOver	Executes a JavaScript code when the mouse cursor is moved into an area (image or link). The mouse cursor must have been outside the area prior to this.
MouseUp	onMouseUp	Executes a JavaScript code when the user releases the mouse key again.
Move	onMove	Executes a JavaScript code when the user or a script moves a window or a frame.
Reset	onReset	Executes a JavaScript code when the user resets a form.
Resize	onResize	Executes a JavaScript code when the user or a script changes the size of a window or frame.
Select	onSelect	Executes a JavaScript code when the user marks an area in a text or text area field.

Event	Event handler	Description
Submit	onSubmit	Executes a JavaScript code when the user submits a form.
Unload	onUnload	Executes a JavaScript when the user exits a document.

Table 1.16 *Overview of all event handlers*

For a detailed description of the event handlers, check the quick reference guide in Section 2.3.

1.9 Forms with JavaScript

If you have already created HTML forms in the past, you will no doubt have been frustrated by the fact that the options for checking the data entered by users were very limited. JavaScript's event handler offers a unique opportunity for checking the basic correctness of the data (e.g. no letters in phone numbers, etc.) on the user's computer before it is even sent. Normally this check can only be carried out with CGI scripts and requires a lot of network resources in many cases. This is because the form containing the incorrect data must first be sent by the user to the server and is then checked for correctness there before the user is prompted to re-enter the correct data. JavaScript enables the data entered to be checked on the user's system, in other words before it is sent over the Internet, so that it only needs to be submitted once by the user.

1.9.1 What is the point of forms?

Forms have an important function in the WWW when it comes to communicating with the user. For example, forms are often used to allow users to register for particular activities or subscribe to particular offers.

1.9.2 Creating forms

Forms are created in the usual way using the normal commands available in HTML.

```
<FORM
ACTION="serverURL"
ENCTYPE="encryptionType"
METHOD="GET"|"POST"
NAME="formName"
onReset="JavaScript code"
```

```
onSubmit="JavaScript code"
TARGET="windowName"
>
...
</FORM>
```

Attribute	Description
`ACTION="serverURL"`	Defines the URL to which the data in the form is to be sent.
`ENCTYPE="enryptionType"`	Indicates the MIME encryption type to be used to send data.
`METHOD="GET" | "POST"`	Defines how the information is to be sent.
`NAME="formName"`	Defines the name of the form.
`onReset="JavaScript-Code"`	Specifies the JavaScript code to be executed as soon as the reset button of the form is pressed.
`onSubmit="JavaScript-Code"`	Specifies the JavaScript code to be executes as soon as the Send button is pressed.
`TARGET="windowName"`	Defines the window in which the data from the form is to be displayed.

Table 1.17 *The* `<FORM>` *tag*

To show you a specific example, let's create a form for receiving subscriptions to a newsletter over the Internet. A serviceable source text for this form might look like this:

```
<HTML>
<HEAD>
<TITLE>Subscribe to Newsletter</TITLE>
</HEAD>
<BODY>
 Please complete this form
 to subscribe to our newsletter.<P>
<FORM NAME="subscribe" METHOD="POST"
ACTION="mailto:my@address.uk" onSubmit="return
check_subscription()">
Surname:<BR>
<INPUT NAME="surname" TYPE="TEXT" SIZE=40><BR>
First name:<BR>
<INPUT NAME="firstname" TYPE="TEXT" SIZE=40><BR>
E-mail:<BR>
```

```
<INPUT NAME="email" TYPE="TEXT" SIZE=50><BR>
<INPUT TYPE="SUBMIT" VALUE="Submit">
<INPUT TYPE="RESET" VALUE="Clear">
</FORM>
</BODY>
</HTML>
```

Once you have saved the form in the JS13 folder under the name sub-scribe.htm, the form looks like this in the browser. Depending on the browser you are using and the version, you may notice some differences.

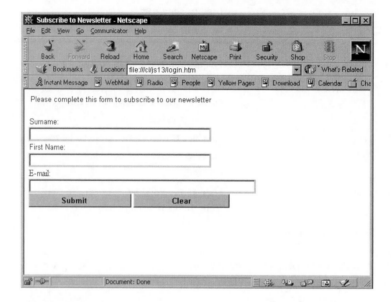

Figure 1.31 *Our form for subscribing to a newsletter*

From a creative viewpoint, this form should not be used in the WWW just like that. However, because this book deals with JavaScript and not with the details of HTML programming and design, it will suffice for our purposes.

As you will have noticed, all input fields and buttons in the form consist of <IN-PUT> tags. But this is an HTML tag, so why have we used it?

Syntax:

```
<INPUT
NAME="inputName"
TYPE="inputType"
VALUE="inputValue"
SIZE=inputSize
MAXLENGTH=inputMaxLength >
```

Attribute	Description
NAME="inputName"	The name of the input field.
TYPE="inputType"	The input field type.
VALUE="inputValue"	The value the input field is to have when loading.
SIZE=inputSize	The characters displayed in the input field.
MAXLENGTH=inputMax-Length	The maximum number of characters the user can enter.

Table 1.18 *The* <INPUT> *tag*

A large number of formula elements can be created using <INPUT>. To tell the browser exactly what kind of information is required here, <INPUT> is always assigned the attribute TYPE. To allow text to be entered you must assign the value TEXT to TYPE. You can define the width of the text field with the SIZE attribute and maximum text length with MAXLENGTH. If you wish, you can even assign a standard value to the text input. This value must be assigned to the VALUE attribute.

```
<INPUT NAME="surname" TYPE="TEXT" SIZE=40 MAXLENGTH=80
VALUE="Smith">
```

This command creates an input field named surname which is 40 characters wide and which permits 80 characters to be entered. When the page appears, the name Smith is already contained in the input field.

Examples of other <INPUT> fields are:

→ Radio buttons (TYPE="RADIO")
→ Check buttons (TYPE="CHECKBOX")
→ Submit button (TYPE="SUBMIT")
→ Reset button (TYPE="RESET")

1.9.3   Evaluating the contents of a form

We want to avoid receiving lots of submissions containing incorrect information, for example errors in the e-mail address. No doubt you will have noticed the check_subscription() function in the listing above. You can use this together with the onSubmit event handler to check the user's input before it is submitted. If the return value of the check_subscription () function is false, then the data in the form is not transferred.

```
function check_subscription()
{
   // To begin with we assume that the submission
   // is correct
   var result = true
```

```
   // The surname input field should contain a value
   if (document.subscribe.surname.value=="")
     {
        alert("Surname missing.")
        result=false
     }


   // Likewise the first name field should also contain a
value
   if (document.subscribe.firstname.value=="")
     {
        alert("First name missing.")
        result=false
     }


   // Check that the e-mail address is OK
   var email = document.subscribe.email.value

   // Is there at least an @ symbol?
   var at_pos

   if (email != "")
      at_pos = email.indexOf("@")
   else
      at_pos = -1

   if (at_pos < 0)
     {
        alert("E-mail address is incorrect: No @-symbol
            entered!")
        result = false
     }
return result
}
```

As soon as our JavaScript has this function, a check runs before the data in the form is transferred to ensure that no obvious errors have crept in during data entry.

check_subscription() is divided into two parts: the examination of the surname and first name and an evaluation of whether the e-mail address contains an @ symbol.

The `var result = true` variable directly at the start of the function allows us to stop the transmission procedure if there is just one single error in one of the input fields.

Let's take a closer look at the examination of the surname and first name.

```
if (document.subscribe.surname.value=="")
  {
     alert("Surname missing.")
     result=false
  }
and
if (document.subscribe.firstname.value=="")
  {
     alert("First name missing.")
     result=false
  }
```

In both cases a check is made here to see whether the input fields for the surname and first name contain any values at all. `document.subscribe.surname.value` refers to the input field of the surname which you have already defined in this section with `<INPUT NAME="surname" TYPE="TEXT" SIZE=40>`. If there is no value in this field (in other words no name), then the `result` variable is set to `false`. The first name is checked in exactly the same way.

The second part of the function ensures that the e-mail address entered is checked to see if it contains an @ symbol.

```
// Check that the e-mail address is OK
   var email = document.subscribe.email.value

   // Is there at least an @ symbol?
   var at_pos

   if (email != "")
      at_pos = email.indexOf("@")
   else
      at_pos = -1

   if (at_pos < 0)
     {
        alert("E-mail address is incorrect: No @ symbol.")
        result = false
     }
```

A check is made here to see if the input field contains an @ symbol. If this condition is met, then this part of the check has been completed successfully. If there is no @ symbol, then the `result` is set to `false`.

If all the fields meet our requirements, then no error message is output and `result` is left unchanged.

1.9.4   Sending the contents of a form

If no errors are found after the contents of the form have been checked, then the data from the form is sent to the address specified with the `<FORM>` tag.

```
<FORM NAME="subscribe" METHOD="POST"
ACTION="mailto:my@address.uk" onSubmit="return
check_subscription()">
```

Here the data is transferred to the `my@address.uk` address.

1.10   Windows and frames

Windows and frames? That's right. The windows and frames that form an integral part of HTML have earned a section to themselves in JavaScript. This is because they are the main area where most JavaScript applications are used. Until now you have only been able to display one page at a time. It would, however, be much more convenient if we could display several pages at once and move them about independently. That's why frames were invented.

1.10.1   Dividing a page into frames

You must create three files in all when you want to divide a page into two frames. The first file defines the size and special features of the two frames. This page is called the frame generating page. The other two files are then loaded to the corresponding parts of the page. In other words each contains the contents of one frame.

First let's look at the file responsible for the structure of the frame. An HTML file of this kind has a normal head, but does not need a body. Instead `<FRAMESET>` ... `</FRAMESET>` is inserted. This tells the browser that a frame is about to be defined.

Because a frame can be divided horizontally or vertically, you should enter one of the following attributes in this tag: `COLS` or `ROWS`. `COLS` defines columns (horizontally separated frames) and `ROWS` defines rows (vertically separated frames).

```
<FRAMESET COLS=20%,80%>
```

In this case, the page would be divided into two columns. The width of the left column would be 20% of the full width of the browser window, while the right hand column would take up the remaining 80%. You can also specify the number of pixels directly. Another option is to use a relative specification in special syntax:

```
<FRAMESET ROWS=40,2*,*>
```

Three rows would be created in this example. The top one would be exactly 40 points high. The two bottom rows would share the rest of the screen in a ratio of 2:1.

Each row or column must now be linked to an HTML page, as otherwise you couldn't display any content. That's why you should insert the `<FRAME>` tag for each frame. The `SRC` attribute can be used to specify the file you want to appear in the frame.

Just in case you're still a bit confused, let's look at an example showing the options provided by a frame. First we need three files to display in the frames. For this you need to create three pages, `a.htm`, `b.htm` and `c.htm`, each of which should only display one letter. So the first page would look like this:

```
<HTML>
  <HEAD>
    <TITLE>A</TITLE>
  </HEAD>
  <BODY>
  A
  </BODY>
</HTML>
```

For the other files you can simply replace the two As with Bs and Cs.

We now need a page that can generate frames. We'll just call it `frame.htm`:

```
<HTML>
  <HEAD>
    <TITLE>Frames example</TITLE>
  </HEAD>
  <FRAMESET ROWS=20%,80%>
    <FRAME SRC="a.htm">
    <FRAME SRC="b.htm">
  </FRAMESET>
</HTML>
```

Figure 1.32 shows the browser display.

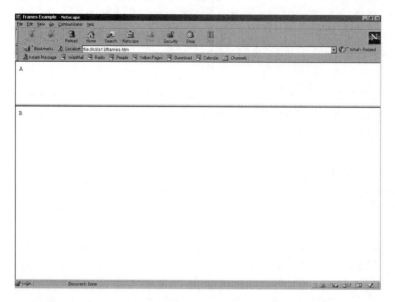

Figure 1.32 *You can display several pages at the same time by defining frames*

You can move the edges of the individual frames in this example as required by simply moving the split bar with the mouse. If you do not want to allow this function to be used, you can insert the <NORESIZE> attribute in FRAME.

You will already have noticed that the browser usually leaves a small blank margin on the sides as well as at the top and bottom. If you want to place text or graphics right at the edge of the frame, you will need a number of other attributes. This is necessary, for example, if the frame is relatively small and is to be filled completely with a graphic. The MARGINHEIGHT attribute therefore defines the size of the upper and lower margin. MARGINWIDTH also allows you to define the side margins. These attributes expect the number of pixels to be defined for the edges. These entries must be greater than zero. This means that the value 1 is the smallest possible frame width.

Of course it can happen that the size of frame is not sufficient to display all information. This is the case, for example, if the frame is too small, the resolution is too low or the content is simply too large. Naturally there is a solution at hand: scroll bars. A browser can also provide these for your frames if necessary. The SCROLLING attribute can be used to define how the browser is to react in relation to these bars. There are three different values for this attribute (see Table 1.19).

Value	Effect
auto	A scroll bar is inserted as required.
yes	A scroll bar is always displayed.
no	No scroll bar is shown, even if one is required.

Table 1.19 *The values of the SCROLLING attribute in frames*

1.10.2 Addressing specific frames

Because the screen now contains several pages at the same time and all of these pages can contain links, you must remember a few things about links in a framed page.

How is the browser to know which page is to appear in which frame and to which page a link refers? It will always follow a simple rule because, unless otherwise specified, a new page always appears in the frame in which the link was activated. So if you insert the following link in the body in the a.htm page, the browser will display the c.htm file in the frame in which the a.htm page previously appeared.

```
<HTML>
  <HEAD>
    <TITLE>A</TITLE>
  </HEAD>
  <BODY>
  A<BR>
  <A HREF="c.htm">Go to page C.</A><BR>
  </BODY>
</HTML>
```

However, in many cases you will want to open a page in a different frame. This is why you can assign a name to each <FRAME>. The NAME attribute is responsible for this. In other words, you could alter the frame.htm file and save it as frame2.htm:

```
<HTML>
  <HEAD>
    <TITLE>Frames example</TITLE>
  </HEAD>
  <FRAMESET ROWS=20%,80%>
    <FRAME SRC="menu1.htm" NAME="menu">
    <FRAME SRC="a.htm" NAME="display">
  </FRAMESET>
</HTML>
```

1.10.3   Menus in a frame page

Now that we have given names to our frames, we can address them easily with JavaScript and implement the following title menu in the frame "menu" for example.

```
<HTML>
  <HEAD>
    <TITLE>Menu</TITLE>
    <SCRIPT LANGUAGE="JavaScript">
    function change(URL) {
      parent.display.location.href = URL;
    }
    </SCRIPT>
  </HEAD>
  <BODY>
  <CENTER>
  <FORM>
    <INPUT TYPE="BUTTON" VALUE="Page A"
onclick="change('a.htm')">
    <INPUT TYPE="BUTTON" VALUE="Page B"
onclick="change('b.htm')">
    <INPUT TYPE="BUTTON" VALUE="Page C"
onclick="change('c.htm')">
  </FORM>
  </CENTER>
  </BODY>
</HTML>
```

Save this file as `menu1.htm` and load `frame2.htm` in your browser. You should now see the window shown in Figure 1.33.

Figure 1.33 *A simple menu using JavaScript*

Sometimes it makes sense to allow the use of the navigation buttons in the menu structure of a web page. We simply use the `History` object for this purpose. As you know, this saves the addresses of the most recently visited web pages and makes them available to JavaScript. A modified version of our menu would therefore look like this:

```
<HTML>
  <HEAD>
    <TITLE>Menu</TITLE>
    <SCRIPT LANGUAGE="JavaScript">
    function change(URL) {
      parent.display.location.href = URL;
    }
    </SCRIPT>
  </HEAD>
  <BODY>
  <CENTER>
  <FORM>
    <INPUT TYPE="BUTTON" VALUE="Previous"
    onclick="parent.display.history.back()">
    <INPUT TYPE="BUTTON" VALUE="Page A"
    onclick="change('a.htm')">
    <INPUT TYPE="BUTTON" VALUE="Page B"
    onclick="change('b.htm')">
    <INPUT TYPE="BUTTON" VALUE="Page C"
```

```
    onclick="change('c.htm')">
    <INPUT TYPE="BUTTON" VALUE="Next"
    onclick="parent.display.history.forward()">
  </FORM>
  </CENTER>
  </BODY>
</HTML>
```

We now see two extra buttons in the menu frame in the browser (Figure 1.34).

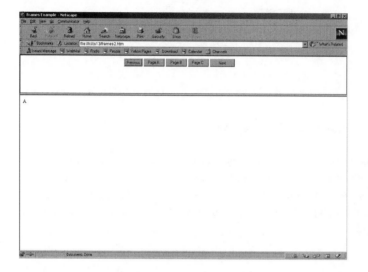

Figure 1.34 *A menu that allows the history object to be used*

The "Next" and "Previous" buttons always cause the browser to move one entry forward or back in the History object. This type of menu guidance system is mainly of interest for web pages that are executed in windows in which the normal Next and Previous buttons are unavailable.

1.10.4 Browsers that do not support frames

Frames have only been introduced in the newer versions of Netscape Navigator and Microsoft Internet Explorer. In other words there are still some older browsers that do not support frames. If a browser of this kind were to encounter a framed page, it would not be able to interpret <FRAME> and would display a blank screen. This is why an extra tag was introduced in all browsers with frame capability in which HTML text is shown which is to be displayed in an old browser. This is called <NOFRAMES> and you can use it as shown in the example below:

```
<HTML>
  <HEAD>
    <TITLE>Frames example</TITLE>
  </HEAD>
  <FRAMESET ROWS=20%,80%>
    <FRAME SRC="menu1.htm" NAME="menu">
    <FRAME SRC="a.htm" NAME="display">
  </FRAMESET>
  <NOFRAMES>
    <HEAD>
      <TITLE>Frames example (unfortunately your browser is
      too old)</TITLE>
    </HEAD>
    <BODY>
      <CENTER>
        CAUTION!<P>
        YOU ARE USING A BROWSER THAT DOES NOT SUPPORT
        FRAMES. CLICK
        <A HREF="a.htm">HERE</A>, FOR A VERSION WITH
        NO FRAMES!<P>
      </CENTER>
    </BODY>
  </NOFRAMES>
</HTML>
```

This browser does not support frames and displays the NOFRAMES section (Figure 1.35).

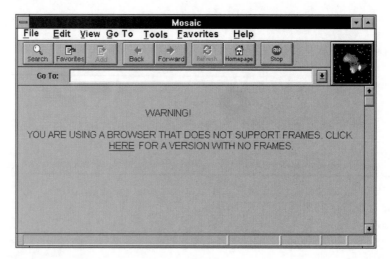

Figure 1.35 *Even though few people use such old browsers it is a good idea to generate this message just in case*

Someone using an old browser will then see the message entered in the <NOF-RAMES> ... </NOFRAMES> area. You can simply insert a link there to a page with no frames.

Part II

Take that!

Quick reference

2

This quick reference guide will provide you with all the information you need to write powerful JavaScript applications. Taken together with the introduction to JavaScript in the previous chapter, it will answer most of your questions as you start to work with JavaScript.

2.1 Objects, methods and properties

This section deals with JavaScript objects, their properties and methods. The abbreviations NS and MS-IE used in the tables of properties and methods refer to Netscape and Microsoft Internet Explorer respectively.

2.1.1   Anchor

`Anchor` allows you to declare a text as a hypertext link within a document. Each object that was created with the HTML `<A>` tag and that supports the `NAME` attribute or that was created using a `String.anchor()` method is stored in the `document.anchors` property. The following syntax is required to define an anchor object by means of the `String.anchor()` method:

`anyString.anchor(nameAttribute)`

If the `Anchor` object is also a link, then the object has an entry in both arrays.

`Anchor` is implemented with effect from JavaScript 1.0 and the following additional properties were added in JavaScript 1.2: `name`, `text`, `x` and `y` (Table 2.1).

Property	NS	JavaScript	read only	static
name	4.0	1.2	X	
text	4.0	1.2	X	
x	4.0	1.2	X	
y	4.0	1.2	X	

Table 2.1 *Properties of* Anchor

The Anchor object inherits the watch() and unwatch() methods from the Object object.

Here is an example of how an Anchor object is created by an HTML <A> tag:

```
<A NAME="first_anchor"><H2>Hello</H2></A>
```

To address an Anchor in another HTML document, you must use the following syntax:

```
<A HREF="hello.html#first_anchor">Hello</A>
```

In this case hello.html is the name of the HTML document.

See also: Link

name

The name property displays the contents of the NAME attribute.

text

The text property contains the text that appears in the <A> tag.

x

The horizontal position of the left corner of the Anchor object relative to the left corner of the document in pixels.

See also: Anchor.y

y

The vertical position of the top corner of the Anchor object relative to the top corner of the document in pixels.

See also: Anchor.x

2.1.2   Applet

An `Applet` object is defined by a normal HTML `<APPLET>` tag. JavaScript creates an entry in the `document.applets[]` array for every `<APPLET>` tag that it finds. To be able to address the `Applet` object, you should assign a value to the `NAME` attribute of the `<APPLET>` tag when creating the object in HTML. You will now have no difficulty finding the `Applet` object you have just created in the array because all you have to do is search for the name.

An `Applet` object inherits all properties defined in the public part of the Java applet.

The same applies to the methods. All methods defined in the public part of the Java applet are inherited from the `Applet` object.

Example:

```
<APPLET CODE="Application.class" WIDTH=220 HEIGHT=100
NAME="myApplication" MAYSCRIPT></APPLET>
```

The `MAYSCRIPT` attribute used in the example is needed to allow JavaScript to access the Java applet. If this attribute is not set, then an error occurs when you try to access the applet with JavaScript.

See also: `MimeType, Plugin`

2.1.3   Area

This defines an area of an image that is to function as an image map. When the user clicks on his part of the image, the hyperlink is loaded in the target window of his browser. `Area` objects are part of the `Link` object.

`Area` has been available with effect from JavaScript 1.1.

See also: `Link`

2.1.4   Array

An array is an ordered group of variables that you can address under one name.

The `Array` object allows you to work with fields under JavaScript. It is available from JavaScript 1.1 onwards and conforms to the ECMA-262 standard.

The following method has been added to the array object with effect from JavaScript 1.3: `toSource()`.

Altered methods from version 1.3 onwards: `push()` and `splice()`.

Altered property in version 1.3: `length`.

An `Array` object can be created in a number of different ways:

By means of the `Array` object `constructor`:

```
new Array(size)
new Array(element0, element1, ...., elementN)
```

An array literal:

```
[element0, element1, ...., elementN]
```

In JavaScript 1.2 when `LANGUAGE= "JavaScript1.2"` is specified in the `<SCRIPT>` tag:

```
new Array(element0, element1, ...., elementN)
```

In JavaScript 1.2 when `LANGUAGE= "JavaScript1.2"` is not specified in the `<SCRIPT>` tag:

```
new Array([size])
new Array([element0[, element1[, ....[, elementN]]]])
```

In JavaScript 1.1:

```
new Array([size])
new Array([element0[, element1[, ....[, elementN]]]])
```

In the examples above, `size` represents the number of elements that the array is to contain when created and `elementN` specifies the values of the various elements. The maximum value of `size` for an array is 4,294,967,295 elements. If you do not specify a number as a parameter when creating the array, then an array with `size` one is created and its first element corresponds to the parameter entered. If you want to create an `Array` object with the elements it is to contain, then `size` is automatically set to the number of elements after the object has been created.

Property	NS	JavaScript	read only	static
constructor	3.0	1.1		
index	4.0	1.2		X
input	4.0	1.2		X
length	3.0	1.1		
prototype	3.0	1.1		

Table 2.2 *Properties of the* `Array` *object*

The `Array` object has the following methods:

Method	NS	JavaScript	static
concat	4.0	1.2	
join	3.0	1.1	
pop	4.0	1.2	
push	4.0	1.2	
reverse	3.0	1.1	
shift	4.0	1.2	
slice	4.0	1.2	
sort	3.0	1.1	
splice	4.0	1.2	
toSource	4.06	1.3	
toString	3.0	1.1	
unshift	4.0	1.2	
valueOf	3.0	1.1	

Table 2.3 *Methods of the* `Array` *object*

The `Array` object also inherits the `watch` and `unwatch` methods of the `object` object.

See also: `image`

concat()

`concat` links two arrays together and returns a new array. The syntax is as follows:

```
concat (arrayName1, arrayName2, ...., arrayNameN)
```

The arrays you link together are not altered when you use `concat`.

constructor

The `constructor` property contains a direct reference to the function created by the prototype of this object. `constructor` conforms to the ECMA-262 standard.

See also: `object.constructor`

index

In the case of an array created by a regular expression, the 0-based index is contained in this property.

input

In the case of an array created by a regular expression, the original string used as the basis for comparison in the regular expression is located here.

join()

join (separator) links all elements of the array in a string and separates these with the character specified in (separator).

The join method conforms to the ECMA-262 standard.

Example:

```
x = new Array("Monday","Tuesday","Wednesday")
myTest1=x.join()
```

Result of this assignment:

```
myTest1="Monday, Tuesday, Wednesday"
myTest2=x.join(, )
```

Result of the second assignment:

```
myTest2="Monday, Tuesday, Wednesday"
myTest3=x.join( - )
```

Result of the last assignment:

```
myTest3="Monday - Tuesday - Wednesday"
```

See also: Array.reverse

length

length returns the number of elements in the array. The maximum number of elements must be less than 2^{32} (i.e. no more than 4,294,967,295). The length property was changed to the above size in JavaScript version 1.3.

The length property also allows you to reduce an array to a required size at any time.

Example:

```
if (myArray.length > 200) {
   myArray.length=200
}
```

pop()

This returns the last element from the array and then deletes it from the array. The pop method is used as shown in the following example:

```
myArray = ["Monday", "Tuesday", "Wednesday", "Thursday",
"Friday", "Saturday", "Sunday"]
myLast = myArray.pop()
```

After this statement `myArray` should contain the following values:

```
myArray = ["Monday", "Tuesday", Wednesday", "Thursday",
"Friday", "Saturday"]
```

and the `myLast` variable should contain the value: `"Sunday"`.

See also: push, shift, unshift

prototype

The `prototype` property stands for the generating function that can be used to add more properties and methods to the defined object. `prototype` conforms to ECMA-272.

Example:

```
myArray.prototype.newProperty = "Value1"
```

See also: Function.prototype

push()

This adds elements to the end of an array and returns the new size of this array.

Example:

```
myArray = ["Monday", "Tuesday", Wednesday", "Thursday",
"Friday"]
newLength = myArray.push("Saturday", "Sunday")
```

After this statement, `myArray` should contain the following value:

```
myNewArray = ["Monday", "Tuesday", "Wednesday", "Thursday",
"Friday", "Saturday", "Sunday"]
```

and the `newLength` variable should contain the value 6.

> **Warning** In JavaScript Version 1.2 push does not return the new size of the array, but just its last element.

See also: pop, shift, unshift

reverse()

`reverse` reverses the order of the elements in the array. The `reverse` method conforms to the ECMA-262 standard.

Example:

```
myArray = new Array("one", "two", "three")
myArray.reverse()
```

When this is applied you get the following result:

`myArray[0]` has the value `"three"`

`myArray[1]` has the value `"two"`

and `myArray[2]` has the value `"one"`.

See also: `Array.join`, `Array.sort`

shift()

The `shift` method enables you to move the first value in an array out of the array and to assign it to a variable. The size of the array is then reduced by one.

Example:

```
myArray = ["Dog", "Cat", "Mouse"]
document.write("myArray previously: " + myArray + "<BR>")
firstElement = myArray.shift()
document.write("myArray subsequently: " + myArray + "<BR>")
document.write("firstElement: " + firstElement + "<BR>")
```

Figure 2.1 shows the output.

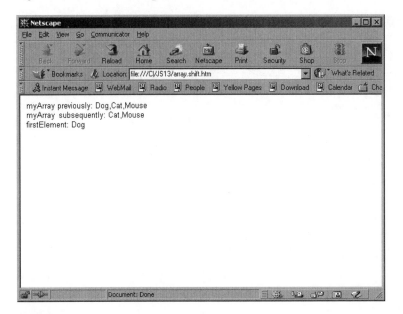

myArray previously: Dog,Cat,Mouse
myArray subsequently: Cat,Mouse
firstElement: Dog

Figure 2.1 *Output from an* `Array.shift()` *method*

See also: `pop`, `push`, `unshift`

slice()

`slice` transfers part of an array to a new array.

Syntax:

```
ArrayObject.slice(start[,end])
```

where `start` stands for the position in the array starting from which the elements are to be entered (inclusively), and `end` represents the position up to which the elements are to be entered (exclusively). It should be noted that the numbering of the positions of the elements starts at element 0. Thus, when the first element in the array is meant, this must be specified with 0.

Example:

```
myArray = ["Dog", "Cat", "Mouse", "House", "Garden"]
document.write("myArray : " + myArray + "<BR>")
newArray = myArray.slice(1,3)
document.write("newArray : " + newArray + "<BR>")
```

Figure 2.2 shows the output on the browser.

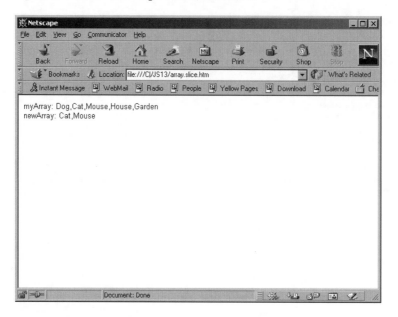

myArray: Dog,Cat,Mouse,House,Garden
newArray: Cat,Mouse

Figure 2.2 *How to use the* `Array.slice()` *method*

When you execute the `slice` method, the array to which you apply `slice` remains unchanged.

sort()

The `sort` method sorts all elements in the array. `sort` conforms to the ECMA-262 standard.

Syntax:

```
ArrayObject.sort(compareFunction)
```

`compareFunction` specifies the sorting sequence for `sort`. If you do not specify a `compareFunction`, then the method will sort in alphabetical order. This means that `"80"` will come before `"9"` in the sorted list. Things are different with a numeric sort; in this case `9` will come before `80`.

Example without `compareFunction`:

```
<SCRIPT>
stringArray = ["Test", "Abra", "Cadabra"]
numberStringArray = ["9", "80", "2", "200"]
numberArray = [8, 70, 11, 112]
mixedNumberArray = ["11", "110", "200", 90, 10, 20]
```

```
function compareFunction (a, b) {
    return a- b
}

document.write("<B>stringArray:</B> " + stringArray +
"<BR>")
document.write("<B>sorts: </B>" + stringArray.sort() +
"<P>")

document.write("<B>numberArray:</B> " + numberArray +
"<BR>")
document.write("<B>sorts without function: </B>" +
numberArray.sort() + "<BR>")
document.write("<B>sorts with function: </B>" +
numberArray.sort(compareFunction) + "<P>")

document.write("<B>numberStringArray:</B> " +
numberStringArray + "<BR>")
document.write("<B>sorts without function: </B>" +
numberStringArray.sort() + "<BR>")
document.write("<B>sorts with function: </B>" +
numberStringArray.sort(compareFunction) + "<P>")

document.write("<B>mixedNumberArray:</B> " +
mixedNumberArray + "<BR>")
document.write("<B>sorts without function: </B>" +
mixedNumberArray.sort() + "<BR>")
document.write("<B>sorts with function: </B>" +
mixedNumberArray.sort(compareFunction) + "<P>")

</SCRIPT>
```

Figure 2.3 shows the browser display resulting from this example.

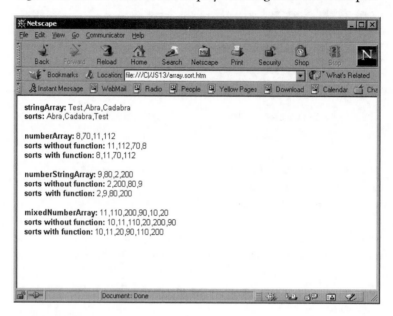

Figure 2.3   *Different kinds of sort with* `Array.sort()`

See also: `Array.join, Array.reverse`

splice()

`splice` changes the content of the array object. New elements are added to the array and old ones are deleted.

Syntax:

```
ArrayObject.splice(index, number, [element1], [....], [ele-
mentN])
```

In this case `index` stands for the position at which changes to the array will start. `number` indicates the number of elements to be deleted. If `number` is specified as `0`, then no elements are removed. `element1, ... , elementN` represents the new elements to be added. If you do not specify any elements to be added, `splice` only deletes the number of elements specified in `number` from an array.

toSource()

`toSource` reproduces the content of the array. This method is normally only used by JavaScript. However, you can use this method to check the content of an array while debugging.

Example:

```
myArray = ["Dog", "Cat", "Mouse"]
Variable = myArray.toSource()
```

After the `toSource` method has run, the value of the `variable` is `["dog",
"cat", "mouse"]`.

See also: `Array.toString`

toString()

The `toString` method returns all elements in an array as a string. `toString`
conforms to the ECMA-262 standard.

Example:

```
myArray = ["Dog", "Cat", "Mouse"]
stringVariable = myArray.toString()
```

After the `toString` method has run, the value of `stringVariable` is
`"dog,cat,mouse"`.

See also: `Array.toSource`

unshift()

`unshift` adds one or more elements to the start of an array and returns the new
length of the array.

Syntax:

```
ArrayObject.unshift(element1, ... , elementN)
```

where `element1, ... , elementN` stands for the elements to be inserted at
the start of the array identified by `ArrayObject`.

See also: `pop`, `push`, `shift`

valueOf()

The elements of the array are converted into strings. The strings are linked together, separated by commas. `valueOf` conforms to ECMA-262 standard.

JavaScript usually only calls `valueOf` internally.

See also: `Object.valueOf`

2.1.5   Boolean

The `Boolean` object is part of the JavaScript core and is available from Java-
Script 1.1 onwards.

The `toSource` method was added to this object in JavaScript version 1.3. This object also conforms to the ECMA-262 standard.

The function of the `Boolean` object is to save a truth value (true or false) and to keep this available for all kinds of evaluations. To create a `Boolean` object you must use the following syntax:

```
myBoolean = new Boolean(value)
```

Here `myBoolean` represents the `Boolean` object to be created and `value` stands for the truth value to be used to initialize `myBoolean`. You can only use `true` or `false` in the code as the truth value.

Table 2.4 lists the properties of the `Boolean` object.

Property	NS	JavaScript	read only	static
constructor	3.0	1.1		
prototype	3.0	1.1		

Table 2.4 *Properties of the* `Boolean` *object*

Table 2.5 lists the methods of the Boolean object.

Method	NS	JavaScript	static
toSource	4.06	1.3	
toString	3.0	1.1	
valueOf	3.0	1.1	

Table 2.5 *Methods of the* `Boolean` *object*

`Boolean` also inherits the `watch` and `unwatch` methods of the `Object` object.

The `Boolean` object is also very interesting for the logic and compare operators.

constructor

The `constructor` property contains a direct reference to the function that creates the prototype of this object. `constructor` conforms to the ECMA-262 standard.

See also: `Object.constructor`

prototype

The `prototype` property represents the generating function of the object which you can use to add more properties and methods to the defined object. `prototype` conforms to ECMA-262.

See also: `Function.prototype`

toSource()

toSource reproduces the contents of the Boolean object. This method is normally only used internally by JavaScript. However, you can also use this method to check the content of a Boolean object while debugging.

See also: Object.toSource

toString()

The toString method returns the value of the Boolean object as a string. toString conforms to the ECMA-262 standard.

Example:

```
var trueOrFalse = new Boolean(true)
var stringVariable = correctOrFalse.toString()
```

The value that appears in the stringVariable variable is "true".

JavaScript automatically uses the toString method when a Boolean object is inserted in a string object.

See also: Object.toString

valueOf()

This converts the elementary value of the Boolean object into a string and returns it. valueOf conforms to the ECMA-262 standard.

valueOf is normally only used internally by JavaScript.

See also: Object.valueOf

2.1.6   Button

You can use the Button object to label HTML buttons in JavaScript. This object allows you to react when the user clicks on an area of the screen. You can also assign or withdraw focus from specific Button objects.

Button has been available since JavaScript 1.0.

Version 1.1 expanded the Button object as follows:

A new type property and new blur and focus methods were added, as well as the event handlers onBlur and onFocus.

From JavaScript version 1.2 onwards the Button object also includes the handleEvent method.

Supported event handlers:

➜ onBlur

➜ onClick
➜ onFocus
➜ onMouseDown
➜ onMouseUp

Table 2.6 shows which properties are supported by the Button object.

Property	NS	JavaScript	read only	static
form	2.0	1.0	X	
name	2.0	1.0		
type	3.0	1.1	X	
value	2.0	1.0	(X)	

Table 2.6 *Properties of the* Button *object*

The methods supported are shown in Table 2.7.

Method	NS	JavaScript	static
blur	2.0	1.0	
click	2.0	1.0	
focus	2.0	1.0	
handleEvent	4.0	1.2	

Table 2.7 *The methods of the* Button *object*

Button also inherits the watch and unwatch methods from the Object object.

Button objects are created for all <INPUT TYPE="BUTTON"> entries found in the HTML document. All buttons in a document are stored in an array in the Form object (Figure 2.4).

See also: Form, Reset, Submit

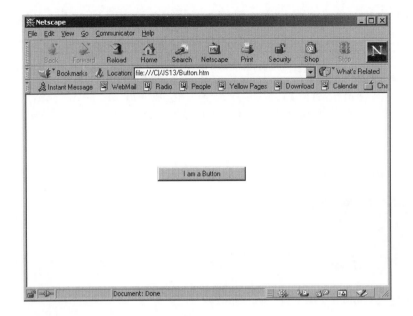

Figure 2.4 *A* Button *object*

blur()

The blur method removes the focus from an object.

Syntax:

```
object.blur()
```

where object stands for a Button object.

See also: Button.focus

click()

click simulates a mouse click on the Button object. click does NOT activate the onClick event handler.

Syntax:

```
object.click()
```

where object stands for a Button object.

focus()

The focus method sets the focus on a Button object.

See also: Button.blur

You can check the form in which the `Button` object is located using this property.

Example:

```
<FORM NAME="Form1">
<INPUT NAME="button1" TYPE="BUTTON" VALUE="Which form con-
tains this button?" onClick="alert('In form:
'+this.form.name)">
</FORM>
```

would return the window shown in Figure 2.5.

Figure 2.5 *Example of the* form *property*

See also: `Form`

handleEvent()

You can use this method to execute a specific event.

Syntax:

```
handleEvent(event)
```

where event stands for the event to be executed.

name

The name of the `Button` object.

type

This displays the `Button` object type.

value

The text displayed on the `Button` object.

Tip This is a read-only property under UNIX and on Macintosh systems.

2.1.7   Checkbox

A Checkbox object in an HTML form.

This object was implemented in JavaScript 1.0.

A Checkbox object is created by the <INPUT> tag in HTML.

Syntax:

```
<INPUT TYPE="CHECKBOX" NAME="testBox" CHECKED> TestBox
```

In Version 1.1, the Checkbox object was expanded as follows:

A new type property and new blur and focus methods were added, as well as the event handlers onBlur and onFocus.

From JavaScript version 1.2 onwards the Checkbox object also includes the handleEvent method.

Supported event handlers:

→ onBlur
→ onClick
→ onFocus

Table 2.8 lists the properties supported by the Checkbox object.

Property	NS	JavaScript	read only	static
checked	2.0	1.0		
defaultChecked	2.0	1.0		
form	2.0	1.0	X	
name	2.0	1.0		
type	3.0	1.1	X	
value	2.0	1.0		

Table 2.8   *Properties of the* Checkbox *object*

Table 2.9 lists the methods supported.

Method	NS	JavaScript	static
blur	2.0	1.0	
click	2.0	1.0	
focus	2.0	1.0	
handleEvent	4.0	1.2	

Table 2.9   *The methods of the* Checkbox *object*

Checkbox also inherits the watch and unwatch methods from the Object object.

Button objects are created for all occurrences of < INPUT TYPE="CHECKBOX" > found in the form. All checkboxes in a document are stored in an array in the Form object.

See also: Form, Radio

blur()

The blur method removes the focus from an object.

Syntax:

```
object.blur()
```

where object stands for a Checkbox object.

See also: Checkbox.focus

checked

This is a Boolean property that indicates the status of the checkbox.

See also: Checkbox.defaultChecked

click()

click simulates a mouse click on the Checkbox object. click does NOT activate the onClick event handler.

Syntax:

```
object.click()
```

where object stands for a Checkbox object.

defaultChecked

This specifies whether or not a Checkbox object is to be checked off by default.

See also: Checkbox.checked

focus()

The focus method sets the focus on a Checkbox object.

See also: Checkbox.blur

form

You can use this property to find out which form contains the Button object.

Example:

```
<FORM NAME="Form1">
<INPUT NAME="checkbox1" TYPE="CHECKBOX" onClick="if
```

```
(this.checked) {alert('In form: '+this.form.name)}"> Do you
want to know which form contains this checkbox?
</FORM>
```

would return the window shown in Figure 2.6.

Figure 2.6   *Example of the* form *property*

See also: Form

handleEvent()

You can use this method to execute specific events.

Syntax:

```
handleEvent(event)
```

where event stands for the event to be executed.

name

The name of the Checkbox object.

type

This displays the Checkbox object type.

value

The value of the Checkbox object.

2.1.8   Date

A Date object allows you to work with date and time values.

This object was implemented in JavaScript 1.0.

A Date object is created with the following constructors:

```
new Date()
new Date(milliseconds)
new Date(year, month, day [, hour, minute, second, milli-
second] )
```

The following constructors are available in JavaScript versions older than 1.3:

```
new Date()
new Date(milliseconds)
new Date(dateString)
new Date(year, month, day [, hour, minute, second] )
```

The Date object has the prototype property with effect from JavaScript version 1.1.

The Checkbox object was extended as follows in version 1.3:

new methods getFullYear, setFullYear, getMilliseconds, setMilliseconds, toSource and UTC.

Table 2.10 lists the properties supported by the Date object.

Property	NS	JavaScript	read only	static
constructor	3.0	1.1		
prototype	3.0	1.1		

Table 2.10 *The properties of the* Date *object*

Table 2.11 lists the methods supported.

Method	NS	JavaScript	static
getDate	2.0	1.0	
getDay	2.0	1.0	
getFullYear	4.06	1.3	
getHours	2.0	1.0	
getMilliseconds	4.06	1.3	
getMinutes	2.0	1.0	
getMonth	2.0	1.0	
getSeconds	2.0	1.0	
getTime	2.0	1.0	
getTimezoneOffset	2.0	1.0	
getUTCDate	4.06	1.3	
getUTCDay	4.06	1.3	
getUTCFullYear	4.06	1.3	
getUTCHours	4.06	1.3	
getUTCMilliseconds	4.06	1.3	
getUTCMinutes	4.06	1.3	
getUTCMonth	4.06	1.3	
getUTCSeconds	4.06	1.3	
getYear	2.0	1.0	
parse	2.0	1.0	X

Method	NS	JavaScript	static
setDate	2.0	1.0	
setFullYear	4.06	1.3	
setHours	2.0	1.0	
setMilliseconds	4.06	1.3	
setMinutes	2.0	1.0	
setMonth	2.0	1.0	
setSeconds	2.0	1.0	
setTime	2.0	1.0	
setUTCDate	4.06	1.3	
setUTCFullYear	4.06	1.3	
setUTCHours	4.06	1.3	
setUTCMilliseconds	4.06	1.3	
setUTCMinutes	4.06	1.3	
setUTCMonth	4.06	1.3	
setUTCSeconds	4.06	1.3	
setYear	2.0	1.0	
toGMTString	2.0	1.0	
toLocaleString	2.0	1.0	
toSource	4.06	1.3	
toString	3.0	1.1	
toUTCString	4.06	1.3	
UTC	2.0	1.0	X
valueOf	3.0	1.1	

Table 2.11 *The methods of the* `Date` *object*

`Date` also inherits the `watch` and `unwatch` methods from the `Object` object.

constructor

The `constructor` property contains a direct reference to the function that creates the prototype of this object. `constructor` conforms to the ECMA-262 standard.

See also: `Object.constructor`

getDate()

This uses a `Date` object to determine the date using local time.

getDay()

This uses a `Date` object to determine the day of the week using local time.

getFullYear()

This uses a `Date` object to determine the year using local time.

getHours()

This returns the value of the hours in a `Date` object using local time.

getMilliseconds()

This returns the value of the milliseconds in a `Date` object using local time.

getMinutes()

This returns the value of the minutes in a `Date` object using local time.

getMonth()

This uses a `Date` object to determine the month using local time.

getSeconds()

This returns the value of the seconds in a `Date` object using local time.

getTime()

This returns the time value of a `Date` object.

getTimezoneOffset()

This returns the time difference in minutes between the host computer and Universal Coordinated Time (UTC).

getUTCDate()

This uses a `Date` object to determine the date using Universal Coordinated Time (UTC).

getUTCDay()

This uses a `Date` object to determine the day of the week using Universal Coordinated Time (UTC).

getUTCFullYear()

This uses a `Date` object to determine the year using the Universal Coordinated Time (UTC).

getUTCHours()

This returns the value of the hours in a `Date` object using Universal Coordinated Time (UTC).

getUTCMilliseconds()

This returns the value of the milliseconds in a `Date` object using Universal Coordinated Time (UTC).

getUTCMinutes()

This returns the value of the minutes in a `Date` object using Universal Coordinated Time (UTC).

getUTCMonth()

This uses a `Date` object to determine the month using Universal Coordinated Time (UTC).

getUTCSeconds()

This returns the value of the seconds in a `Date` object using Universal Coordinated Time (UTC).

getYear()

This returns the value of the year in a `Date` object.

parse()

Parses the supplied date string and returns the date value.

prototype

This returns a reference to the prototype of an object class.

setDate()

This sets the numeric date of the `Date` object using local time.

setFullYear()

This sets the value of the year in a `Date` object using the local time.

setHours()

This sets the value in hours in the `Date` object using the local time.

setMilliseconds()

This sets the value in milliseconds in the `Date` object using the local time.

setMinutes()

This sets the value in minutes in the `Date` object using the local time.

setMonth()

This sets the value of the month in the Date object using the local time.

setSeconds()

This sets the value of the seconds in the Date object using the local time.

setTime()

This sets the values of the date and time in the Date object.

setUTCDate()

This sets the numeric date in the Date object using Universal Coordinated Time (UTC).

setUTCFullYear()

This sets the year in the Date object using Universal Coordinated Time (UTC).

setUTCHours()

This sets the hours value in the Date object using Universal Coordinated Time (UTC).

setUTCMilliseconds()

This sets the milliseconds value in the Date object using Universal Coordinated Time (UTC).

setUTCMinutes()

This sets the minutes value in the Date object using Universal Coordinated Time (UTC).

setUTCMonth()

This sets the value of the month in the Date object using Universal Coordinated Time (UTC).

setUTCSeconds()

This sets the value of the seconds in the Date object using Universal Coordinated Time (UTC).

setYear()

This sets the value of the year in the Date object.

toGMTString()

This uses GMT (Greenwich Mean Time) to return the date converted into a string.

toLocaleString()

This uses local time to return the date converted into a string.

toSource()

`toSource` reproduces the content of the `Date` object. This method is normally only used by JavaScript. However, you can use this method to check the contents of a `Date` object while debugging.

See also: `Object.toSource`

toString()

The `toString` method returns the value of the `Date` object as a string. `toString` conforms to the ECMA-262 standard.

See also: `Object.toString`

toUTCString()

This uses Universal Coordinated Time (UTC) to return the date converted into a string.

UTC()

This returns the numeric representation of the time specified by the entered values.

valueOf()

This converts the elementary value of the `Date` object into a string and returns it. `valueOf` conforms to the ECMA-262 standard.

`valueOf` is normally only called internally by JavaScript.

See also: `Object.valueOf`

2.1.9   Document

The `Document` object contains all the key information the browser needs to be able to display the data on an HTML page for the user.

This object was implemented in JavaScript 1.0.

A `Document` object is created by the `<BODY>` tag in HTML.

In version 1.1 the `Document` object was expanded as follows:

The `applets`, `domain`, `embeds`, `forms`, `formName`, `images` and `plugins` properties are new.

From JavaScript version 1.2 onwards the `Document` object also has the following properties: `classes`, `ids`, `layers` and `tags`. The `captureEvents`, `contextual`, `getSelection`, `handleEvents`, `releaseEvents` and `routeEvents` methods were added.

Supported event handlers:

→ `onClick`
→ `onDblClick`
→ `onKeyDown`
→ `onKeyPress`
→ `onKeyUp`
→ `onMouseDown`
→ `onMouseUp`

Table 2.12 lists the properties supported by the `Document` object.

Property	NS	JavaScript	read only	static
alinkColor	2.0	1.0		
anchors	2.0	1.0	X	
applets	3.0	1.1	X	
bgColor	2.0	1.0		
classes	4.0	1.2		
cookie	2.0	1.0		
domain	3.0	1.1		
embeds	3.0	1.1	X	
fgColor	2.0	1.0		
forms	3.0	1.1	X	
height	4.0	1.2		
ids	4.0	1.2		
images	3.0	1.1	X	
lastModified	2.0	1.0	X	
layers	4.0	1.2		
linkColor	2.0	1.0		
links	2.0	1.0	X	
plugins	3.0	1.1	X	
referrer	4.0	1.2		
tags	4.0	1.2		
title	2.0	1.0	X	
URL	2.0	1.0	X	

Property	NS	JavaScript	read only	static
vlinkColor	2.0	1.0		
width	4.0	1.2		

Table 2.12 *The properties of the* Document *object*

Table 2.13 lists the supported methods.

Method	NS	JavaScript	static
captureEvents	4.0	1.2	
close	2.0	1.0	
contextual	4.0	1.2	
getSelection	4.0	1.2	
handleEvent	4.0	1.2	
open	2.0	1.0	
releaseEvents	4.0	1.2	
routeEvent	4.0	1.2	
write	2.0	1.0	
writeln	2.0	1.0	

Table 2.13 *The methods of the* Document *object*

Document also inherits the watch and unwatch methods from the Object object.

See also: Frame, window

alinkColor

This sets the color a link turns when a user clicks it.

See also: document.bgColor, document.fgColor, document.linkColor, document.vlinkColor

anchors

The array containing the Anchor objects defined on this page.

applets

The array containing the Applet objects defined on this page.

bgColor

Sets the background color for this page.

See also: document.alinkColor, document.fgColor, document.linkColor, document.vlinkColor

captureEvents()

captureEvents captures events as they arise and transfers them to the Document object.

Syntax:

`captureEvents(event)`

If you want to capture several events, you should separate them with OR (|).

classes

This defines style classes

See also: `document.contextual`, `document.ids`, `document.tags`, `Style`

close()

This closes a document. Not to be confused with the `window.close()` method. `document.close()` closes the output channel to a document previously opened with `document.open()`.

See also: `document.open`, `document.write`, `document.writeln`

contextual()

This defines a context-dependent style.

Syntax:

`contextual(style1, style2, ...)`

See also: `document.classes`, `document.tags`, `Style`

cookie

The cookies associated with the current document.

See also: `Hidden`

domain

The domain name of the server from which the displayed document originates.

embeds

The array containing the Embed objects defined on this page.

See also: `Plugin`

fgColor

The foreground color of this page.

See also: document.alinkColor, document.bgColor, document.linkColor, document.vlinkColor

forms

The array containing the Form objects defined on this page.

getSelection()

The text currently highlighted in the document is returned using this method.

handleEvent()

You can use this method to execute a specific event.

Syntax:

handleEvent(event)

where event stands for the event to be executed.

height

The height of the document displayed.

See also: document.width.

ids

Defines the style of individual tags.

See also: document.contextual, document.classes, document.tags, Style

images

The array containing the Image objects defined on this page.

lastModified

This property contains the date of the last change to the document.

layers

The array containing the Layer objects defined on this page.

linkColor

Defines the color of links before they are clicked.

See also: `document.alinkColor`, `document.bgColor`, `document.fgColor`, `document.vlinkColor`

links

The array containing the `Link` objects defined on this page.

open()

This opens a document. After it has been opened, you can use `document.write()` to write data into the document. `document.close()` closes the output channel to the document.

See also: `document.close`, `document.write`, `document.writeln`, `Location.reload`, `Location.replace`

plugins

The array containing the `Plugin` objects defined on this page.

referrer

The URL of the page by means of which a user reaches this page. If the user enters the link directly and has not reached this page by clicking a link, then this property does not have a value.

releaseEvents()

`releaseEvents` ends the capturing of events as they arise.

Syntax:

`releaseEvents(event)`

If several events are no longer to be captured, you must separate them with OR characters (|).

routeEvent()

This routes captured events to the normal event hierarchy.

tags

This defines the style of HTML tags.

See also: `document.classes`, `document.contextual`, `document.ids`, `Style`

title

The text displayed in the browser title bar when the document is opened.

URL

The complete URL of the page displayed.

See also: `Location.href`

vlinkColor

This sets the color of already visited links.

See also: `document.alinkColor, document.bgColor, document.fgColor, document.linkColor`.

width

This sets the width of the document displayed.

See also: `document.height`

write()

This writes strings to the document.

See also: `document.close, document.open, document.writeln`

writeln()

This writes strings to the document and appends a line feed at the end of the string.

See also: `document.close, document.open, document.write`

2.1.10   event

The `event` object contains all the key information required by the browser in order to process user events.

This object was implemented in JavaScript 1.2.

An `event` object is created when an event handler is activated.

Table 2.14 lists the properties supported by the `document` object.

Property	NS	JavaScript	read only	static
data	4.0	1.2		
height	4.0	1.2		
layerX	4.0	1.2		
layerY	4.0	1.2		
modifiers	4.0	1.2		
pageX	4.0	1.2		
pageY	4.0	1.2		

Property	NS	JavaScript	read only	static
screenX	4.0	1.2		
screenY	4.0	1.2		
target	4.0	1.2		
type	4.0	1.2		
which	4.0	1.2		
width	4.0	1.2		
x	4.0	1.2		
y	4.0	1.2		

Table 2.14 *The properties of the* event *object*

event also inherits the watch and unwatch methods from the Object object.

data

An array with strings containing the URLs of objects placed in the browser window using the Drag&Drop technique.

height

Indicates the height of the frame or window in which the event was activated.

See also: event.width

layerX

Contains the x coordinates of the event that has occurred relative to the Layer object in which the event was activated.

See also: event.layerY

layerY

Contains the y coordinates of the event that has occurred relative to the Layer object in which the event was activated.

See also: event.layerX

modifiers

This property indicates whether other keys have been pressed. Possible values:

→ SHIFT_MASK
→ CONTROL_MASK
→ ALT_MASK
→ META_MASK

See also: event.which

pageX

This contains the x coordinates of the event that has occurred relative to the top left corner of the document in which the event was activated.

See also: `event.pageY`

pageY

This contains the y coordinates of the event that has occurred relative to the top left corner of the document in which the event was activated.

See also: `event.pageX`

screenX

This contains the absolute x coordinates of the event that has occurred.

See also: `event.screenY`

screenY

This contains the absolute y coordinates of the event that has occurred.

See also: `event.screenX`

target

The object used to activate the event.

See also: `event.type`

type

Indicates which event has occurred.

See also: `event.target`

which

Indicates the ASCII code of the pressed key or mouse button. In the case of the mouse buttons, 1 stands for the left button, 2 for the middle button and 3 for the right hand button.

See also: `event.modifiers`

width

The width of the window or frame in which the event was activated.

See also: `event.height`

x

See `layerX`

y

See `layerY`

2.1.11   FileUpload

The `FileUpload` object provides a dialog for specifying file names which is displayed for the user in the typical way for his or her operating system.

This object was implemented in JavaScript 1.0.

A `FileUpload` object is created using the HTML command `<INPUT TYPE="FILE">` in a form.

The `type` property was added to the `FileUpload` object in version 1.1.

From JavaScript version 1.2 onwards, the `FileUpload` object also includes the `handleEvent` method.

Supported event handlers:

→ `onBlur`
→ `onChange`
→ `onFocus`

Table 2.15 lists the properties supported by the `FileUpload` object.

Property	NS	JavaScript	read only	static
form	2.0	1.0	X	
name	2.0	1.0	X	
type	3.0	1.1	X	
value	2.0	1.0	X	

Table 2.15   *The properties of the* `FileUpload` *object*

Table 2.16 lists the methods supported.

Method	NS	JavaScript	static
blur	2.0	1.0	
focus	2.0	1.0	
handleEvent	4.0	1.2	
select	2.0	1.0	

Table 2.16   *The methods of the* `FileUpload` *object*

The `FileUpload` object also inherits the `watch` and `unwatch` methods of the `Object` object.

See also: `Text`.

blur()

The blur method removes the focus from an object.

Syntax:

Object.blur()

where Object stands for a FileUpload object.

See also: FileUpload.focus, FileUpload.select

focus()

The focus method sets the focus on a FileUpload object.

See also: FileUpload.blur, FileUpload.select

form

You can check which form contains the FileUpload object using this property.

See also: Form

handleEvent()

You can use this method to execute specific events.

Syntax:

handleEvent(event)

where event stands for the event to be executed.

name

The name of the FileUpload object.

select()

This highlights the text entered in the FileUpload object.

See also: FileUpload.blur, FileUpload.focus

type

This displays the FileUpload object type.

value

The value of the FileUpload object.

2.1.12   Form

The `Form` object contains all the key information required by the browser in order to be able to display a form for the user.

This object was implemented in JavaScript 1.0.

A `Form` object is created by the `<FORM>` tag in HTML.

The `reset` method was added to the `Form` object in version 1.1.

From JavaScript version 1.2 onwards, the `Form` object also includes the `handleEvent` method.

Supported event handlers:

→ `onReset`
→ `onSubmit`

Table 2.17 lists the properties supported by the `Form` object.

Property	NS	JavaScript	read only	static
action	2.0	1.0		
elements	2.0	1.0	X	
encoding	2.0	1.0		
length	2.0	1.0	X	
method	2.0	1.0		
name	2.0	1.0		
target	2.0	1.0		

Table 2.17   *The properties of the* `form` *object*

Table 2.18 lists the methods supported.

Method	NS	JavaScript	static
handleEvent	4.0	1.2	
reset	3.0	1.1	
submit	2.0	1.0	

Table 2.18   *The methods of the* `Form` *object*

The `Form` object also inherits the `watch` and `unwatch` methods from the `Object` object.

See also: `Button, Checkbox, document.forms, FileUpload, Hidden, Password, Radio, Reset, Select, Submit, Text, Textarea`

action

The `action` attribute of the `<FORM>` tag.

elements

The array containing all objects of the form.

encoding

The type of encryption to be used by the form for its data.

handleEvent()

This method allows you to execute specific events.

Syntax:

`handleEvent(event)`

where `event` stands for the event to be executed.

length

The syntax

`document.forms.length`

displays the number of forms in the document, where

`document.forms[1].length`

displays the number of elements in this particular form.

method

Corresponds to the `method` attribute of the `<FORM>` tag.

name

The name of the form.

reset()

Discards all entries made by the user and restores the initialization values of the form.

submit()

Submits the content of the form without the user needing to click on a submit button. To prevent data from being sent without being noticed, the user is informed of the transfer by means of a message box.

target

Corresponds to the `target` attribute of the `<FORM>` tag.

2.1.13   Frame

Frame allows you to divide a window into several smaller windows. All frames defined in a document can be found under `document.frames`. For a more detailed description of this object, please check out the `window` object as these two objects are very similar.

2.1.14   Function

The `Function` object enables you to create a function under JavaScript by transferring a string to the object.

This object was implemented in JavaScript 1.1.

A `Function` object is created by the following constructor:

```
Function(arg1, arg2, ..., argN, code)
```

where `arg1, arg2, ..., argN` stand for the transfer values to the new `Function` object and `code` stands for the JavaScript code it is to contain.

The `Function` object was expanded as follows in version 1.2:

The `arity`, `arguments` and `callee` properties are new.

With effect from JavaScript version 1.3, the `Function` object also includes the `apply-`, `call` and `toSource` methods. The `arguments.caller` property was removed.

Table 2.19 lists the properties supported by the `Function` object.

Property	NS	JavaScript	read only	static
arguments	3.0	1.1		
arguments.callee	4.0	1.2		
arguments.caller	3.0	1.1		
arguments.length	3.0	1.1		
arity	4.0	1.2		
constructor	3.0	1.1		
length	4.0	1.1		
prototype	4.0	1.1		

Table 2.19   *The properties of the* `Function` *object*

Table 2.20 lists the methods supported.

Method	NS	JavaScript	static
apply	4.06	1.3	
call	4.06	1.3	
toSource	4.06	1.3	
toString	3.0	1.1	
valueOf	3.0	1.1	

Table 2.20 *The methods of the* Function *object*

apply()

Calls up the function as a method of an object.

Syntax:

```
apply(object, arg1, arg2, ..., argN)
```

In this case object stands for the object whose method is to call this function. The values in arg1, arg2, ..., argN are entered as transfer values for the method.

See also: Function.call

arguments

The transfer values entered for the function.

arguments.callee

This returns the content of the function.

See also: Function.arguments

arguments.caller

The function that called this function.

See also: Function.arguments

arguments.length

The number of transfer values entered for the function.

See also: Function.arguments

arity

This specifies the expected number of transfer values from this function.

See also: arguments.length, Function.length

call()

This enables you to execute a different function within another function. The special feature of `call` is that the called function acts as if it were the calling function, so that all values assigned with `this` are set in the calling function rather than the called one.

See also: `Function.apply`

constructor

The `constructor` feature contains a direct reference to the function that creates the prototype of this object. `constructor` conforms to the ECMA-262 standard.

See also: `Object.constructor`

length

This indicates the number of arguments the function expects.

See also: `arguments.length`

prototype

The `prototype` property stands for the generating function of the object for assigning more properties and methods to the defined object. `prototype` conforms to the ECMA-262 standard.

Example:

```
object.prototype.newProperty = "value1"
```

where `object` stands for the object to which you add the new property or method.

See also: `Function.prototype`

toSource()

`toSource` displays the contents of the `function` object. This method is normally only used by JavaScript. However, you can also use this method to check the contents of a `function` object while debugging.

See also: `Object.toSource`

toString()

The `toString` method returns the value of the `function` object as a string. `toString` conforms to the ECMA-262 standard.

See also: `Object.toString`

valueOf()

This converts the elementary value of the `function` object into a string and returns it. `valueOf` conforms to the ECMA-262 standard.

`valueOf` is normally only called internally by JavaScript.

See also: `Object.valueOf`

2.1.15 Hidden

The `Hidden` object is a `Text` object which the user cannot see. It is mainly used to store data temporarily without displaying it to the user in this form.

This object was implemented in JavaScript 1.0.

A `Hidden` object is created with the `<INPUT>` tag in HTML.

```
<INPUT
   TYPE="HIDDEN"
   NAME="elementHiddenName"
   [VALUE="stdValue"]>
```

In this case the `HIDDEN` type stands for the `Hidden` object, `elementHidden-Name` stands for the name to be assigned to the object, and `stdValue` stands for the default value to be used to initialize this object.

The `Hidden` object was expanded to include the `type` property in version 1.1.

Table 2.21 lists the properties supported by the `Hidden` object.

Property	NS	JavaScript	read only	static
form	2.0	1.0	X	
name	2.0	1.0		
type	3.0	1.1		
value	2.0	1.0		

Table 2.21 *The properties of the* `Hidden` *object*

`Hidden` inherits the `watch` and `unwatch` methods from the `Object` object.

`Hidden` objects are created for every `<INPUT TYPE="HIDDEN">` found in the form. All hidden text fields contained in a form are stored in an array in the `Form` object.

See also: `document.cookie`

form

You can use this property to find out which form contains the Hidden object.

See also: Form

name

The name of the Hidden object.

type

This has the value "hidden" for all Hidden objects. This property indicates the object type.

value

The text containing the Hidden object.

2.1.16   History

The History object contains all the most recently visited pages in the browser.

This object was implemented in JavaScript 1.0.

The History object was expanded as follows in version 1.1:

The current, next and previous properties are new.

Table 2.22 lists the properties supported by the History object.

Property	NS	JavaScript	read only	static
current	3.0	1.1	X	
length	2.0	1.0	X	
next	3.0	1.1	X	
previous	3.0	1.1	X	

Table 2.22   *The properties of the* History *object*

Table 2.23 lists the methods supported.

Method	NS	JavaScript	static
back	2.0	1.0	
forward	2.0	1.0	
go	2.0	1.0	

Table 2.23   *The methods of the* History *object*

History inherits the watch and unwatch methods from the Object object.

See also: `Location`, `Location.replace`

back()

Goes back one element in the History list.

See also: `History.forward`, `History.go`

current

Displays the URL of the user's current page.

See also: `History.next`, `History.previous`

forward()

Moves forward one element in the History list.

See also: `History.back`, `History.go`

go()

Syntax:

`go(number)`

This moves `number` elements forward if the value is positive, and `number` elements back if the number is negative.

See also: `History.back`, `History.forward`, `Location.reload`, `Location.replace`

length

The number of elements in the `History` object.

next

The URL of the next page in the History list.

See also: `History.current`, `History.previous`

previous

The URL of the previous page in the History list.

See also: `History.current`, `History.next`

2.1.17   Image

An `Image` object represents an image on the HTML page.

This object was implemented in JavaScript 1.1.

An `Image` object is created by means of the `<IMG>` tag in HTML or the following constructor:

```
new Image([width,] [height])
```

The `Image` object was expanded to include the `handleEvent` method in version 1.2.

Supported event handlers:

→ `onAbort`
→ `onError`
→ `onKeyDown`
→ `onKeyPress`
→ `onKeyUp`
→ `onLoad`

Table 2.24 lists all properties supported by the `Image` object.

Property	NS	JavaScript	read only	static
border	3.0	1.1	X	
complete	3.0	1.1	X	
height	3.0	1.1	X	
hspace	3.0	1.1	X	
lowsrc	3.0	1.1		
name	3.0	1.1	X	
src	3.0	1.1		
vspace	3.0	1.1	X	
width	3.0	1.1	X	

Table 2.24 *The properties of the* `Image` *object*

Table 2.25 lists the supported methods:

Method	NS	JavaScript	static
handleEvent	4.0	1.2	

Table 2.25 *The methods of the* `Image` *object*

The `Image` object also inherits the `watch` and `unwatch` methods from the `Object` object.

You can create `Image` objects for every `<IMG>` tag found on the HTML page.

See also: `Link`, `onClick`, `onMouseOut`, `onMouseOver`

border

The width of the frame

See also: `Image.height`, `Image.hspace`,
`Image.vspace`, `Image.width`

complete

When the image is fully loaded, the value of this property is `true`.

See also: `Image.lowsrc`, `Image.src`

handleEvent()

This method allows you to execute specific events.

Syntax:

`handleEvent(event)`

where `event` stands for the event to be executed.

height

The height of the image in pixel.

See also: `Image.border`, `Image.hspace`,
`Image.vspace`, `Image.width`

hspace

The horizontal space between the image and the surrounding objects on the HTML page.

See also: `Image.border`, `Image.height`,
`Image.vspace`, `Image.width`

lowsrc

URL for a lower resolution version of the image.

See also: `Image.complete`, `Image.src`

name

The name of the `Image` object.

src

URL for an image to be displayed in the HTML document.

See also: `Image.complete`, `Image.lowsrc`

vspace

The vertical space between the image and the surrounding objects on the HTML page.

See also: `Image.border, Image.height,`
`Image.hspace, Image.width`

width

The width of the image in pixels.

See also: `Image.border, Image.height,`
`Image.hspace, Image.vspace`

2.1.18   java

A top-level object, used to address any class in the `java.*` package.

See also: `Packages, Packages.java`

2.1.19   JavaArray

The `JavaArray` object contains all the key information you will need to administer JavaArrays.

This object was implemented in Core-JavaScript 1.1.

Any Java method that returns an array can create a `JavaArray` object.

Table 2.26 lists the properties supported by the `JavaArray` object.

Property	NS	JavaScript	read only	static
length	3.0	1.1		

Table 2.26   *The properties of the* `JavaArray` *object*

Table 2.27 lists the methods supported.

Method	NS	JavaScript	static
toString	3.0	1.1	

Table 2.27   *The methods of the* `JavaArray` *object*

length

The number of elements in the array displayed by the `JavaArray` object.

See also: `Array.length`

toString()

The `toString` returns the value of the `JavaArray` object as a string.

See also: `Object.toString`

2.1.20   JavaClass

A JavaScript reference to a Java class.

This object was implemented in core JavaScript 1.1.

You create a `JavaClass` object by calling a Java class in a package. `JavaClass` saves the name of the Java class.

The properties of the `JavaClass` object are the statistical fields of the Java class.

As methods the `JavaClass` object contains the statistical methods of the Java class.

See also: `JavaArray, JavaObject, JavaPackage, Packages`

2.1.21   JavaObject

A `JavaObject` object is created by every Java method that returns an object.

The properties of the `JavaObject` object are the public fields of the Java class, from which it forms an instance. In addition, all public fields of the superclasses also create properties.

The methods of the `JavaObject` object are the public methods of the Java class used to form an instance. In addition, all methods of `java.lang` and all other superclasses also create methods.

See also: `JavaArray, JavaClass, JavaPackage, Packages`

2.1.22   JavaPackage

A JavaScript reference to a Java package.

This object was implemented in core JavaScript 1.1.

A `JavaPackage` object is created by calling a Java class in a package. `JavaPackage` saves the name of the package.

The properties of the `JavaPackage` object are the Java classes and all the other packages that this package contains.

See also: `JavaArray, JavaClass, JavaObject, Packages`

2.1.23 Layer

The Layer object contains all the key information required by the browser in order to display layers on HTML pages for the user.

This object was implemented in JavaScript 1.2.

A Layer object is created by the <LAYER> tag or the <ILAYER> tag in HTML, by means of cascading style sheets with the <SPAN> or <DIV> tag or by means of the constructor of the Layer object.

Supported event handlers:

→ onBlur
→ onFocus
→ onLoad
→ onMouseOut
→ onMouseOver

Table 2.28 lists the properties supported by the Layer object.

Property	NS	JavaScript	read only	static
above	4.0	1.2	X	
background	4.0	1.2		
below	4.0	1.2	X	
bgColor	4.0	1.2		
clip.bottom	4.0	1.2		
clip.heigth	4.0	1.2		
clip.left	4.0	1.2		
clip.right	4.0	1.2		
clip.top	4.0	1.2		
clip.width	4.0	1.2		
document	4.0	1.2	X	
left	4.0	1.2		
name	4.0	1.2	X	
pageX	4.0	1.2		
pageY	4.0	1.2		
parentLayer	4.0	1.2		
siblingAbove	4.0	1.2	X	
siblingBelow	4.0	1.2	X	
src	4.0	1.2		
top	4.0	1.2		
visibility	4.0	1.2		
window	4.0	1.2	X	

Property	NS	JavaScript	read only	static
x	4.0	1.2		
y	4.0	1.2		
zIndex	4.0	1.2		

Table 2.28 *The properties of the* Layer *object*

Table 2.29 lists the methods supported.

Method	NS	JavaScript	static
captureEvents	4.0	1.2	
handleEvent	4.0	1.2	
load	4.0	1.2	
moveAbove	4.0	1.2	
moveBelow	4.0	1.2	
moveBy	4.0	1.2	
moveTo	4.0	1.2	
moveToAbsolute	4.0	1.2	
releaseEvents	4.0	1.2	
resizeBy	4.0	1.2	
resizeTo	4.0	1.2	
routeEvent	4.0	1.2	

Table 2.29 *The methods of the* Layer *object*

Layer also inherits the watch and unwatch methods from the Object object.

You should use the <DIV> tag to create Layer objects instead of the <Layer> and <ILAYER> tags.

above

The Layer object with the next highest zIndex. If the current Layer object already has the highest zIndex, then above points to the window object.

background

The background image of the Layer object.

below

The Layer object with the next lowest zIndex. If current Layer object is already the lowest zIndex, then the value of below is zero.

bgColor

The background color.

captureEvents()

`captureEvents` captures events as they occur and transfers them to the `Layer` object.

Syntax:

`captureEvents(event)`

If several events are to be captured, then you must separate them with OR characters (|).

clip.bottom

The y coordinates of the bottom edge of the clipping area.

clip.height

The height of the clipping area.

clip.left

The x coordinates of the left edge of the clipping area.

clip.right

The x coordinates of the right edge of the clipping area.

clip.top

The y coordinates of the top edge of the clipping area

clip.width

The width of the clipping area.

document

The `document` object displayed in the `Layer` object.

handleEvent()

This method allows you to execute specific events.

Syntax:

`handleEvent(event)`

where `event` stands for the event to be executed.

left

The horizontal position of the top left corner of the `Layer` object in pixels relative to the position of the higher layer.

load()

Loads a new document in the Layer object.

Syntax:

```
load(URL, width)
```

URL stands for the URL of the document to be loaded and width stands for the width in pixels.

moveAbove()

This increases the zIndex until the Layer object is displayed by means of the Layer object.

Syntax:

```
moveAbove(layer)
```

where layer stands for the Layer object by means of which the current layer is to be displayed.

moveBelow()

This reduces the zIndex until the current Layer object is displayed under the specified Layer object.

Syntax:

```
moveBelow(layer)
```

where layer stands for the Layer object under which the current layer is to be displayed.

moveBy()

This moves the layer object relative to its present position.

moveTo()

This moves the top left corner of the Layer object to the specified screen coordinates relative to the higher Layer object.

Syntax:

```
moveTo(xcoordinate, ycoordinates)
```

moveToAbsolute()

Moves the top left corner of the Layer object to the specified screen coordinates relative to the browser window.

Syntax:

```
moveToAbsolute(xcoordinate, ycoordinates)
```

name

The name of the `Layer` object.

pageX

The x coordinates relative to the browser window.

pageY

The y coordinates relative to the browser window.

parentLayer

The higher `Layer` object.

releaseEvents()

`releaseEvents` halts the capture of events as they arise.

Syntax:

```
releaseEvents(event)
```

If you want to halt the capture of several events, then you must separate these using OR (|).

resizeBy()

Changes the size of the `Layer` object relative to the current size.

Syntax:

```
resizeBy(relativewidth, relativeheight)
```

resizeTo()

Changes the size of the `Layer` object.

Syntax:

```
resizeTo(width, height)
```

routeEvent()

Routes captured events to the normal event hierarchy.

siblingAbove

Returns the `Layer` object with the next highest `zIndex` from the set of all `Layer` objects that share the same `parentLayer`. If there is no `siblingAbove` for this `Layer` object, the value returned is `zero`.

siblingBelow

Returns the `Layer` object with the next lowest `zIndex` from the set of all `Layer` objects that share the same `parentLayer`. If there is no `siblingBelow` for this `Layer` object, the value returned is `zero`.

src

The URL of the document displayed in the `Layer` object.

top

The y coordinates of the `Layer` object relative to its `parentLayer`.

visibility

This specifies whether the `Layer` object is visible. If the value is `"show"` or `"visible"` then the `Layer` object is displayed. It is not displayed if the value is `"hide"`. If the value set is `"inherit"` then visibility follows from the setting for the higher `Layer` object.

window

The `window` or `Frame` object containing the `Layer` object.

x

The x coordinates of the `Layer` object.

y

The y coordinates of the `Layer` object.

zIndex

Specifies the sequence in which the `Layer` objects are to be cascaded. A parent `zIndex` means that the `Layer` object is displayed above a `Layer` object with a lower `zIndex`.

2.1.24   Link

The `Link` object represents a link in an HTML document. All hyperlinks in an HTML page are defined in the `documents.links` array and can be queried there.

The Link object was introduced in JavaScript 1.0; the onMouseOut event handler was added in version 1.1.

The properties x, y and text are new since JavaScript 1.2. The handleEvent method was also added in this version.

Table 2.30 lists the properties supported by the Link object.

Property	NS	JavaScript	read only	static
hash	2.0	1.0		
host	2.0	1.0		
hostname	2.0	1.0		
href	2.0	1.0		
pathname	2.0	1.0		
port	2.0	1.0		
protocol	2.0	1.0		
search	2.0	1.0		
target	2.0	1.0		
text	4.0	1.2		
x	4.0	1.2	X	
y	4.0	1.2	X	

Table 2.30 *The properties of the* Link *object*

When it comes to the properties you should note that x, y, and text are **not** available with Microsoft Internet Explorer but are only supported by Netscape.

Method	NS	JavaScript	static
handleEvent	4.0	1.2	

Table 2.31 *The methods of the* Link *object*

Link also inherits the watch and unwatch methods from the Object object.

The Link object supports the following objects:

→ onClick
→ onDblClick
→ onKeyDown
→ onKeyPress
→ onKeyUp
→ onMouseDown
→ onMouseOut
→ onMouseUp
→ onMouseOver

A Link object is created in the HTML document using the usual commands in HTML.

```
<A HREF="url"
    [NAME="anchor_name"]
    [TARGET="window_name"]
    [onClick="handler_code_click"]
    [onDblClick="handler_code_dblclick"]
    [onMouseOut="handler_code_onmouseout"]
    [onMouseOver="handler_code_onmouseover"]
    [onMouseDown="handler_code_onmousedown"]
    [onMouseUp="handler_code_mouseup"]> link_text </A>
```

See also: Anchor and Image

handleEvent()

This starts the specified event handler for the specified event.

Syntax:

```
handleEvent(event)
```

event stands for the event handler to be executed.

hash

This specifies the anchor of a link. The anchor is specified in HTML with the # symbol.

See also: Link.host, Link.hostname, Link.href, Link.pathname, Link.port, Link.protocol, Link.search

host

This specifies the host name and the port separated by a colon. If no port is specified, then no colon is submitted.

See also: Link.hash, Link.hostname, Link.href, Link.pathname, Link.port, Link.protocol, Link.search

hostname

The name of the server to which the link refers.

See also: Link.hash, Link.host, Link.href, Link.pathname, Link.port, Link.protocol, Link.search

href

The complete link with all specifications.

See also: `Link.hash`, `Link.host`, `Link.hostname`, `Link.pathname`, `Link.port`, `Link.protocol`, `Link.search`

pathname

This displays the path and file to which a link refers.

See also: `Link.hash`, `Link.host`, `Link.hostname`, `Link.href`, `Link.port`, `Link.protocol`, `Link.search`

port

The port to which the link is connected.

See also: `Link.hash`, `Link.host`, `Link.hostname`, `Link.href`, `Link.pathname`, `Link.protocol`, `Link.search`

protocol

The protocol used for this link. The value `"ftp:"` is stored here for an FTP link, while the value for an HTTP link is `"http:"`.

See also: `Link.hash`, `Link.host`, `Link.hostname`, `Link.href`, `Link.pathname`, `Link.port`, `Link.search`

search

This specifies the search string for a URL. The search string is specified directly after the normal URL. To indicate that a search string is to follow, this is introduced by a ?.

See also: `Link.hash`, `Link.host`, `Link.hostname`, `Link.href`, `Link.pathname`, `Link.port`, `Link.protocol`

target

The value stored in the `<A TARGET>` tag can be found here again.

See also: `Form`

text

The text of the link.

x

The x coordinate of the link.

See also: `Link.y`

y

The y coordinate of the link.

See also: Link.x

2.1.25 Location

The Location object contains information about the URL for the current HTML page.

This object was implemented in JavaScript 1.0.

A Location object is automatically created for every window object.

The document object was expanded as follows in version 1.1:

The reload and replace methods were added.

A URL is constructed according to the following scheme:

protocol//hostname:port/pathname#hash?search

protocol can contain the values listed in Table 2.32.

protocol	URL type
javascript:	JavaScript code
view-source:	Netscape source code viewer
about:	Netscape information
http:	WWW
file:	File system
ftp:	FTP
mailto:	E-mail
news:	News server
gopher:	Gopher services

Table 2.32 Protocols for URLs

Table 2.33 lists the properties supported by the Location object.

Property	NS	JavaScript	read only	static
hash	2.0	1.0		
host	2.0	1.0		
hostname	2.0	1.0		
href	2.0	1.0		
pathname	2.0	1.0		
port	2.0	1.0		
protocol	2.0	1.0		

Property	NS	JavaScript	read only	static
search	2.0	1.0		

Table 2.33 *The properties of the* Location *object*

Table 2.34 lists the supported methods.

Method	NS	JavaScript	static
reload	3.0	1.1	
replace	3.0	1.1	

Table 2.34 *The methods of the* Location *object*

Location also inherits the watch and unwatch methods from the Object object.

See also: History, document.URL

hash

This specifies the anchor of a link. The anchor is indicated by the # character in HTML.

See also: location.host, Location.hostname, Location.href, Location.pathname, Location.port, Location.protocol, Location.search

host

This specifies the name of the host and the port separated by a colon. If there is no port specified, then there is no colon.

See also: location.hash, Location.hostname, Location.href, Location.pathname, Location.port, Location.protocol, Location.search

hostname

The name of the server to which the link refers.

See also: location.hash, Location.host, Location.href, Location.pathname, Location.port, Location.protocol, Location.search

href

The complete link with all specifications.

See also: `location.hash`, `Location.host`, `Location.hostname`, `Location.pathname`, `Location.port`, `Location.protocol`, `Location.search`

pathname

This shows the path and file to which a link refers.

See also: `location.hash`, `Location.host`, `Location.hostname`, `Location.href`, `Location.port`, `Location.protocol`, `Location.search`

port

The port to which the link is connected.

See also: `location.hash`, `Location.host`, `Location.hostname`, `Location.href`, `Location.pathname`, `Location.protocol`, `Location.search`

protocol

The protocol used for this link. In the case of an FTP connection, the value `"ftp:"` would be stored here, while in the case of an HTTP connection, the value would be `"http:"`.

See also: `location.hash`, `Location.host`, `Location.hostname`, `Location.href`, `Location.pathname`, `Location.port`, `Location.search`

reload()

This method forces the browser to reload a page from the server. A Boolean expression can be entered as an option. This indicates whether the server is to load the page even if it is already contained in the browser cache. To force transfer, you must specify `true`.

See also: `location.replace`

replace()

`replace` allows you to exit the browser, load a new page and to replace the previous page in the history with the page you have just called. As a result, the user does not return to the page where they clicked a link.

See also: `History`, `History.go`, `location.reload`, `window.open`

search

This specifies the search string of a URL. The search string appears directly after the normal URL. To indicate that a search string is to follow, the string is introduced by a ?.

See also: `Location.hash`, `Location.host`, `Location.hostname`, `Location.href`, `Location.pathname`, `Location.port`, `Location.protocol`

2.1.26   Math

The `Math` object contains properties and methods that provide constants and functions for mathematical calculations.

This object was implemented in JavaScript 1.0 and conforms to the ECMA-262 standard.

A `Math` object is generated automatically.

Table 2.35 lists the properties supported by the `Math` object.

Property	NS	JavaScript	read only	static
E	2.0	1.0	X	X
LN10	2.0	1.0	X	X
LN2	2.0	1.0	X	X
LOG10E	2.0	1.0	X	X
LOG2E	2.0	1.0	X	X
PI	2.0	1.0	X	X
SQRT1_2	2.0	1.0	X	X
SQRT2	2.0	1.0	X	X

Table 2.35   *The properties of the* `Math` *object*

Table 2.36 lists the methods supported by the `Math` object.

Method	NS	JavaScript	static
abs	2.0	1.0	X
acos	2.0	1.0	X
asin	2.0	1.0	X
atan	2.0	1.0	X
atan2	2.0	1.0	X
ceil	2.0	1.0	X
cos	2.0	1.0	X
exp	2.0	1.0	X
floor	2.0	1.0	X

Method	NS	JavaScript	static
log	2.0	1.0	X
max	2.0	1.0	X
min	2.0	1.0	X
pow	2.0	1.0	X
random	2.0	1.0	X
round	2.0	1.0	X
sin	2.0	1.0	X
sqrt	2.0	1.0	X
tan	2.0	1.0	X

Table 2.36 *All methods of the* Math *object*

Math also inherits the watch and unwatch methods from the Object object.

abs()

This returns the absolute value of a number.

acos()

This returns the arc cosine in radians of a number (the value is the length of the arc).

See also: Math.asin, Math.atan, Math.atan2, Math.cos, Math.sin, Math.tan

asin()

This returns the arc sine in radians of a number (the value is the length of the arc).

See also: Math.acos, Math.asin, Math.atan, Math.atan2, Math.cos, Math.sin, Math.tan

atan()

This returns the arctangent in radians of a number (the value is the length of the arc).

See also: Math.acos, Math.asin, Math.atan2, Math.cos, Math.sin, Math.tan

atan2()

This returns the arc tangent. The correct syntax for this method is:

```
atan2(os, as)
```

`os` stands for the opposite side and `as` stands for the adjacent side. The result returned is the angle at the adjacent side.

See also: `Math.acos`, `Math.asin`, `Math.atan`, `Math.cos`, `Math.sin`, `Math.tan`

ceil()

Rounds a number up to its next highest integer.

See also: `Math.floor`

cos()

This returns the cosine of a number in radians.

See also: `Math.acos`, `Math.asin`, `Math.atan`, `Math.atan2`, `Math.sin`, `Math.tan`

E

The Eulerian number e which roughly corresponds to the value 2.7182818284590451.

exp()

`exp(x)` returns the value of e^x.

See also: `Math.E`, `Math.log`, `Math.pow`

floor()

This rounds a number to the next lowest integer.

See also: `Math.ceil`

LN10

The natural logarithm of 10, i.e. roughly the value 2.302585092994045684017991454 68436.

LN2

The natural logarithm of 2. The value corresponds roughly to 0.6931471805599453094172321214 58177.

log()

`log(x)` returns the logarithm of x in base e. If x <= 0, then the method returns the value -1.797693134862316e+308.

See also: `Math.exp`, `Math.pow`

LOG10E

This returns the logarithm of the Eularian constant e in base 10, so that the constant corresponds roughly to the value 0.434.

LOG2E

This returns the logarithm of the Eularian constant e in base 2.

max()

This returns the higher value of two specified numeric expressions.

See also: `Math.min`

min()

This returns the lesser of two specified numeric expressions.

See also: `Math.max`

PI

The number π, approximately 3.1415926535897931.

pow()

Returns the value of an expression raised to the power of the specified index. `pow(x,y)` returns the result of x to the power of y.

See also: `Math.exp`, `Math.log`

random()

This returns a random number between 0 and 1 which is determined by means of the time. This function only worked in UNIX systems in JavaScript 1.0, but since JavaScript 1.1 it runs on all platforms.

round()

Rounds the specified number up or down. Rounding follows mathematical rules: numbers larger than 5 in the decimal place are rounded up, while numbers less than 5 are rounded down.

sin()

Returns the sine in radians of a number.

See also: `Math.acos`, `Math.asin`, `Math.atan`, `Math.atan2`, `Math.cos`, `Math.tan`

sqrt()

This calculates the square root of the specified number. If a minus number has been specified, then this method returns the value 0.

SQRT1_2

The square root of 0.5.

SQRT2

The square root of 2.

tan()

Returns the tangent in radians of a number.

See also: `Math.acos`, `Math.asin`, `Math.atan`, `Math.atan2`, `Math.cos`, `Math.sin`

2.1.27   MimeType

The `MimeType` object contains the MIME types supported by the browser.

This object was implemented in JavaScript 1.1.

Table 2.37 lists the properties supported by the `document` object.

Property	NS	JavaScript	read only	static
description	3.0	1.1	X	
enabledPlugin	3.0	1.1	X	
suffixes	3.0	1.1	X	
type	3.0	1.1	X	

Table 2.37 *The properties of the* `MimeType` *object*

The `MimeType` object inherits the `watch` and `unwatch` methods from the `Object` object.

description

A description of the MIME type.

enabledPlugin

A reference to the plugin object that supports this MIME type. If the MIME type is not supported by a plugin, then this property is assigned the value `zero`.

suffixes

A string with possible file extensions for this MIME type, separated by commas.

type

The name of the MIME type.

2.1.28   navigator

The `navigator` object contains all the key information about the browser used.

This object was implemented in JavaScript 1.0.

The `navigator` object is automatically created by the JavaScript runtime engine.

The `navigator` object was expanded as follows in version 1.1:

The `mimeTypes` and `plugins` properties and the `javaEnabled` and `taintEnabled` methods were added.

With effect from JavaScript version 1.2, the `navigator` object also includes the `language` and `platform` properties. The `preference` and `savePreferences` methods were added.

Table 2.38 lists the properties supported by the `navigator` object.

Property	NS	JavaScript	read only	static
appCodeName	2.0	1.0	X	
appName	2.0	1.0	X	
appVersion	2.0	1.0	X	
language	4.0	1.2	X	
mimeTypes	3.0	1.1	X	
platform	4.0	1.2	X	
plugins	3.0	1.1	X	
userAgent	2.0	1.0	X	

Table 2.38   *The properties of the* `navigator` *object*

Table 2.39 lists the methods supported.

Method	NS	JavaScript	static
javaEnabled	3.0	1.1	X
plugins.refresh			
preference	4.0	1.2	X
savePreference	4.0	1.2	X
taintEnabled	3.0	1.1	X

Table 2.39 *The methods of the* navigator *object*

navigator also inherits the watch and unwatch methods from the Object object.

appCodeName

The code name of the browser.

appName

The name of the browser.

appVersion

The browser version. The version is stored in the following format:

versionNumber (platform; country)

where the appVersion property could subsequently contain a string such as:

3.0 (Win95, I)

In this case I stands for the international version of the browser and U stands for the US version. Different encryption procedures are supported in US versions.

javaEnabled()

This method returns the value true if the browser used is suitable for Java. If the browser is not suitable for Java, then the value returned is false. A false value is also returned if the user has disabled Java capability in his browser.

See also: navigator.appCodeName, navigator.appName, navigator.userAgent

language

The abbreviation for the language version of the browser en indicates the English version.

mimeTypes

The array containing information about the MIME types supported by the browser.

See also: `MimeType`

platform

This contains a string indicating the platform for which this browser was written. Possible values are: Win32, Win16, Mac68k, MacPPC and various UNIX versions.

plugins

An array containing information about the installed plugins.

plugins.refresh()

This makes newly installed plugins available to the browser while it is running. The method can be assigned a Boolean value indicating whether the update is to affect already open documents.

preference()

This allows you to set and read user settings. Because it accesses security-related data, this method is only available in signed scripts.

See also: `savePreference`

savePreference()

This saves the user settings for the browser. This method is only available in signed scripts.

See also: `preference`

taintEnabled()

`taintEnabled` was implemented in Netscape Navigator 3.0 on an experimental basis and is no longer available from JavaScript version 1.2 onwards. This method indicates whether or not data tainting is available.

See also: `taint, untaint`

userAgent

The full name of the browser; also used when logging on to a web server.

2.1.29   netscape

A top-level object which is required in order to be able to use Java classes in the `netscape.*` package.

This object was implemented in core JavaScript 1.1.

The `netscape` object does not need to be created separately because it is predefined. It can be used without needing to call a constructor or method first.

See also: `Packages`, `Packages.netscape`

2.1.30   Number

The `Number` object contains all the key information that JavaScript needs to process numbers.

This object was implemented in JavaScript 1.1 and conforms to the ECMA-262 standard.

A `Number` object is created by the constructor of the `Number` object.

Syntax:

```
new Number(value)
```

The `Number` object was expanded as follows in version 1.3:

The `toSource` method is new.

Table 2.40 lists the properties supported by the `Number` object.

Property	NS	JavaScript	read only	static
constructor	3.0	1.1		
MAX_VALUE	3.0	1.1	X	X
MIN_VALUE	3.0	1.1	X	X
NaN	3.0	1.1	X	
NEGATIVE_INFINITY	3.0	1.1	X	X
POSITIVE_INFINITY	3.0	1.1	X	X
prototype	3.0	1.1		

Table 2.40 *The properties of the* `Number` *object*

Table 2.41 lists the methods supported.

Method	NS	JavaScript	static
toSource	4.06	1.3	
toString	3.0	1.1	
valueOf	3.0	1.1	

Table 2.41 *The methods of the* Number *object*

document also inherits the watch and unwatch methods from the Object object.

constructor

The constructor property contains a direct reference to the function that creates the prototypes of this object. constructor conforms to the ECMA-262 standard.

See also: Object.constructor

MAX_VALUE

The largest number you can use in JavaScript.

MIN_VALUE

The smallest number you can use in JavaScript.

NaN

Indicates that the value to be processed is not a number.

NEGATIVE_INFINITY

Indicates negative infinity.

POSITIVE_INFINITY

Indicates positive infinity.

prototype

The prototype property represents the generating function of the object. You can use this to add more properties and methods to the defined object. prototype conforms to the ECMA-262 standard.

See also: Function.prototype

toSource()

toSource returns the content of the Number object. This method is normally only used by JavaScript. However, you can use this method to check the content of a Number object while debugging.

See also: Object.toSource

toString()

The toString method returns the value of the Number object as a string. toString conforms to the ECMA-262 standard.

See also: Object.toString

valueOf()

The elementary value of the Number object is converted to a sequence of characters and returned. valueOf conforms to the ECMA-262 standard.

valueOf is normally only called internally by JavaScript.

See also: Object.valueOf

2.1.31   Object

The Object object is the basic object of all JavaScript objects and all other objects in JavaScript are derived from it.

This object was implemented in JavaScript 1.0 and conforms to the ECMA-262 standard.

An Object object is created by its constructor.

Syntax:

```
new Object()
```

The Object object was expanded as follows in version 1.1:

The constructor property and the eval and valueOf methods are new.

The eval method was removed again in JavaScript version 1.2.

With effect from JavaScript version 1.3 the Object object also includes the toSource method.

Table 2.42 lists the properties supported by the `Object` object.

Property	NS	JavaScript	read only	static
constructor	3.0	1.1		
prototype	3.0	1.1		

Table 2.42 *The properties of the* `Object` *object*

Table 2.43 lists the methods supported.

Method	NS	JavaScript	static
eval	3.0	1.1	
toSource	4.06	1.3	
toString	2.0	1.0	
unwatch	4.0	1.2	
valueOf	3.0	1.1	
watch	4.0	1.2	

Table 2.43 *The methods of the* `Object` *object*

constructor

The constructor method of an object

eval()

You can use this method, which is only implemented in Netscape Navigator 3.0, to execute submitted JavaScript code. `eval` is a global function in other browser versions.

prototype

This allows you to add methods and properties to all JavaScript objects.

toSource()

`toSource` returns the content of the object in the form of a string. You can use this string to make a copy of the object.

See also: `Object.toString`

toString()

The `toString` method returns the value of the object as a string. `toString` conforms to the ECMA-262 standard.

See also: `Object.toSource`, `Object.valueOf`

unwatch()

This deactivates the watch (property) statement.

valueOf()

This converts the elementary value of the object into a string and returns it. valueOf conforms to the ECMA-262 standard.

See also: parseInt, Object.toString

watch()

This allows you to monitor a particular property and to react with a handler when the property changes. The syntax for watch is:

```
watch(property, handler)
```

where property stands for the property you want to monitor and handler stands for the function to be called when a change occurs.

2.1.32   Option

The Option object is used to display option lists in JavaScript.

This object was implemented in JavaScript 1.0.

An Option object is created by means of the <OPTION> tag in HTML or by means of its constructor:

Syntax:

```
new Option([text[, value[, standardSelection[, selected]]]])
```

The Option object was expanded to include the defaultSelected property in version 1.1.

Table 2.44 lists the properties supported by the Option object.

Property	NS	JavaScript	read only	static
defaultSelected	3.0	1.1		
index	2.0	1.0		
length	2.0	1.0	X	
selected	2.0	1.0		
text	2.0	1.0		
value	2.0	1.0	X	

Table 2.44   *The properties of the* Option *object*

Option inherits the watch and unwatch methods from the Object object.

defaultSelected

The element to be selected by default.

index

The number of the entry in the list of selection options.

length

The number of entries in the options list.

selected

This is `true` if the queried element in the list is selected.

text

The text of an element that can be selected in the options list.

value

The value following the element to be selected. This does not have to be the text of the element, but can be set as required. For example, this value is sent with e-mail in the case of forms.

2.1.33   Packages

A top-level object required in order to be able to use Java classes in `Packages`.

This object was implemented in core JavaScript 1.1.

You do not need to create the `Packages` object separately because it is predefined. You can use it without first having to call a constructor or a method.

Table 2.45 lists the properties supported by the `Packages` object.

Property	NS	JavaScript	read only	static
className	3.0	1.1		
java	3.0	1.1		
netscape	3.0	1.1		
sun	3.0	1.1		

Table 2.45   *The properties of the* `Packages` *object*

className

The full name of the Java class which is not defined in the `netscape`, `java` or `sun` classes of JavaScript.

java

All classes of the `java.*` Java class.

netscape

All classes of the `netscape.*` Java class.

sun

All classes of the `sun.*` Java class.

2.1.34 Password

The `Password` object contains all the information the browser needs to be able to display and use a password field on an HTML page.

This object was implemented in JavaScript 1.0.

A `Password` object is created by the `<INPUT TYPE="PASSWORD">` tag in HTML.

The `Password` object was expanded as follows in version 1.1:

The `type` property and the `onBlur` and `onFocus` event handlers are new.

With effect from JavaScript version 1.2, the `Password` object also includes the `handleEvent` method.

Supported event handlers:

→ `onBlur`
→ `onFocus`

Table 2.46 lists the properties supported by the `Password` object.

Property	NS	JavaScript	read only	static
defaultValue	2.0	1.0		
form	2.0	1.0		
name	2.0	1.0		
type	3.0	1.1	X	
value	2.0	1.0		

Table 2.46 *The properties of the* `Password` *object*

Table 2.47 lists the supported methods.

Method	NS	JavaScript	static
blur	2.0	1.0	
focus	2.0	1.0	
handleEvent	4.0	1.2	
select	2.0	1.0	

Table 2.47 *The methods of the* `Password` *object*

`Password` also inherits the `watch` and `unwatch` methods from the `Object` object.

See also: `Form`, `Text`

blur()

This deactivates the `Password` object.

defaultValue

The default value for the `Password` object when created.

focus()

This sets the focus on the `Password` object.

form

Link to the `Form` object where the `Password` object is located.

handleEvent()

This method allows you to execute specific events.

Syntax:

`handleEvent(event)`

where `event` stands for the event to be executed.

name

The name of the `Password` object.

select()

This highlights the text entered in a `Password` object.

type

The type of the `Password` object. The default here is `"password"`.

value

The value of the `Password` object. The value specified in `value` will be contained here immediately after the page is loaded.

2.1.35   Plugin

The `Plugin` object contains data about plugins installed on the user's system.

This object was implemented in JavaScript 1.1.

`Plugin` objects are predefined JavaScript objects which can be checked in the `navigator.plugins` array.

Table 2.48 lists the properties supported by the `Plugin` object.

Property	NS	JavaScript	read only	static
description	3.0	1.1	X	
filename	3.0	1.1	X	
length	3.0	1.1	X	
name	3.0	1.1	X	

Table 2.48   *The properties of the* `Plugin` *object*

`Plugin` also inherits the `watch` and `unwatch` methods from the `Object` object.

See also: `MimeType`, `document.embeds`.

description

A description of the plugin.

filename

The name of the file containing the plugin.

length

This property contains the number of MIME types supported by this `Plugin` object.

name

The name of the plugin. The value of this property is also contained in the `plugins[]` array in the `navigator` object.

2.1.36 Radio

The `Radio` object contains all the information the browser needs to be able to work with a group of radio buttons.

This object was implemented in JavaScript 1.0.

A `Radio` object is created by means of the `<INPUT TYPE="RADIO">` tag in HTML.

In version 1.1 the `Radio` object was expanded as follows:

The `type` property and the `onBlur` and `onFocus` event handlers were added.

With effect from JavaScript version 1.2, the `Radio` object also includes the `handleEvent` method.

Supported event handlers:

→ `onBlur`
→ `onClick`
→ `onFocus`

Table 2.49 lists the properties supported by the `Radio` object.

Property	NS	JavaScript	read only	static
checked	2.0	1.0		
defaultChecked	2.0	1.0		
form	2.0	1.0	X	
name	2.0	1.0		
type	3.0	1.1	X	
value	2.0	1.0	X	

Table 2.49 *The properties of the* `Radio` *object*

Table 2.50 lists the methods supported.

Method	NS	JavaScript	static
blur	2.0	1.0	
click	2.0	1.0	
focus	2.0	1.0	
handleEvent	4.0	1.2	

Table 2.50 *The methods of the* `Radio` *object*

`Radio` also inherits the `watch` and `unwatch` methods from the `Object` object.

See also: `Checkbox, Form, Select`

blur()

This deactivates the Radio object.

checked

This specifies whether a Radio object is marked. Because the Radio object can contain more than just a radio button, the various buttons must be addressed using an array index.

click()

click simulates a mouse click on the Radio object. click does NOT activate the onClick event handler.

Syntax:

```
Object.click()
```

where Object stands for a Radio object.

defaultChecked

The radio button to be selected when the Radio object is displayed for the first time.

focus()

This sets the focus on the Radio object.

form

Refers to the Form object containing the Radio object.

handleEvent()

This method allows you to execute specific events.

Syntax:

```
handleEvent(event)
```

where event stands for the event to be executed.

name

The name of the Radio object.

type

The type of the Radio object. Default "radio".

value

The value of a radio button.

2.1.37　RegExp

The RegExp object allows you to search for particular patterns in strings.

This object was implemented in JavaScript 1.2.

A RegExp object is created by constructors.

Syntax:

literal notation:

`/text/flags`

by means of the normal constructor:

`new RegExp("text"[, "flags"])`

In both options `text` stands for the regular expression to be matched and `flags` stands for the various types of search. Possible values for `flags` are as follows:

g　= global match

i　= ignore case

gi = global match and ignore case

In version 1.3 the RegExp object was expanded to include the `toSource` method.

The regular expression supports the following syntax.

Reserved characters	Description
\	Backslash.
^	Matches the start of the text.
$	Matches the end of the text.
*	Previous expression should match 0 times or more (means the same as {0, }).
+	Previous expression should match 1 time or more (means the same as {1, }).
?	Previous expression should match 0 or 1 time (means the same as {0,1}).
.	Any character except \n.
(x)	Searches for x and groups the match.
x|y	Searches for x or y.
{n}	Character should occur exactly n times.

Reserved characters	Description
{n,}	Character should occur at least n times.
{n,m}	Character should occur at least n times but no more than m times.
[xyz]	Matches any characters within the set of characters specified. For example " [a-z] " would only match lowercase characters and " [abcdef] " would only match lowercase letters a, b, c, d, e, or f.
[^xyz]	Matches the character not in the set.
\b	Matches a word limit, i.e. the position between a word and a blank. For example "er\b" corresponds to the "er" in "painter", but not to the "er" in "verb".
\B	Matches a non-word limit. "ee*r\B" corresponds to the "eer" in "Beers".
\d	Matches a digit. Equivalent to [0-9].
\D	Matches a non-digit. Equivalent to [^0-9].
\f	Matches a page break character.
\n	Matches a line break character.
\r	Matches a carriage return character.
\s	Matches any empty spaces, such as blanks, tabs, page break, etc. Equivalent to " [\f\n\r\t\v] ".
\S	Matches any non-empty spaces. Equivalent to " [^ \f\n\r\t\v] ".
\t	Matches a tab character.
\v	Matches a vertical tab.
\w	Matches all alphabetical characters, including underscore. Equivalent to " [A-Za-z0-9_] ".
\W	Matches all non-alphabetical characters. Equivalent to " [^A-Za-z0-9_] ".
\num	Corresponds to group num if num is a positive integer. " (.)\1" corresponds to two identical characters in consecutive sequence.
\onum	Matches onum where onum is an octal escape value. Octal escape values can have 1, 2 or 3 places. For example, both "\11" and "\011" corresponds to the tab character. "\0011" is equivalent to "\001" & "1". Octal escape values may not exceed 256, as otherwise only the first two places contain the expression. This allows you to use ASCII codes in regular expressions.

Reserved characters	Description
\xnum	Matches xnum, where xnum is a hexadecimal escape value. Hexadecimal escape values can only have two places. For example, "\x41" corresponds to "A". "\x041" is equivalent to "\x04" & "1". This allows you to use ASCII codes in regular expressions.

Table 2.51 *Special characters in* RegExp

Table 2.52 lists the properties supported by the RegExp object.

Property	NS	JavaScript	read only	static
$1,...,$9	4.0	1.2	X	X
$_				
$*				
$&				
$+				
$`				
$´				
constructor	3.0	1.1		
global	4.0	1.2	X	
ignoreCase	4.0	1.2	X	
input	4.0	1.2		X
lastIndex	4.0	1.2		
lastMatch	4.0	1.2	X	X
lastParen	4.0	1.2	X	X
leftContext	4.0	1.2	X	X
multiline	4.0	1.2		X
prototype	3.0	1.1		
rightContext	4.0	1.2	X	X
source	4.0	1.2	X	

Table 2.52 *The properties of the* RegExp *object*

Table 2.53 lists the methods supported.

Method	NS	JavaScript	static
compile	4.0	1.2	
exec	4.0	1.2	
test	4.0	1.2	
toSource	4.06	1.3	
toString	3.0	1.1	

Method	NS	JavaScript	static
valueOf	3.0	1.1	

Table 2.53 *The methods of the* RegExp *object*

The RegExp object also inherits the watch and unwatch methods from the Object object.

$1,...,$9

This contains the last nine group matches.

$_

Means the same as input.

$*

Means the same as multiline.

$&

Means the same as lastmatch.

$+

Means the same as lastParen.

$`

Means the same as leftContext.

$´

Means the same as rightContext.

compile()

Compiles the specified regular expression.

Syntax:

```
compile(text, flags)
```

You can only use this method if the RegExp object was created with a constructor.

constructor

The constructor property contains the direct reference to the function that creates the prototype of this object. constructor conforms to the ECMA-262 standard.

See also: `Object.constructor`

exec()

This applies the regular expression to the string submitted to the `exec` method.

global

Indicates whether the `g` flag was used.

ignoreCase

Indicates whether the `i` flag was used.

input

The string to which the regular expression was applied.

lastIndex

The location in the text where the last match ended.

lastMatch

The characters matched by the last expression.

lastParen

This contains the characters found in the last match by means of a parenthetical expression.

leftContext

Everything to the left of the last substring found.

multiline

Indicates whether the search is to cover more than one line. `multiline` contains a Boolean value.

prototype

The `prototype` property stands for the generating function of the object which can be used to add more properties and methods to the defined object. `prototype` conforms to the ECMA-262 standard.

See also: `Function.prototype`

rightContext

Everything to the right of the last substring found.

source

This contains the expression searched for without \ or g or i.

test()

This checks whether the regular expression matches the string entered. The method returns `true` for a match and `false` for no match.

toSource()

`toSource` returns the content of the `RegExp` object. This method is normally only used by JavaScript. However you can use this method to check the contents of a `RegExp` object while debugging.

See also: `Object.toSource`

toString()

The `toString` method returns the value of the `RegExp` object as a string. `toString` conforms to the ECMA-262 standard.

See also: `Object.toString`

valueOf()

The elementary value of the `RegExp` object is converted to a sequence of characters and returned. `valueOf` conforms to the ECMA-262 standard.

`valueOf` is normally only called internally by JavaScript.

See also: `Object.valueOf`

2.1.38   Reset

The `Reset` object stands for a reset button in a form on a website.

This object was implemented in JavaScript 1.0.

A `Reset` object is created by the `<INPUT TYPE="RESET">` tag in HTML.

The `Reset` object was expanded as follows in version 1.1:

The `type` property and the `blur` and `focus` methods were added. In addition, the `onBlur` and `onFocus` event handlers were introduced.

With effect from JavaScript version 1.2 the `Reset` object also includes the `handleEvent` method.

Supported event handlers:

➔ `onBlur`
➔ `onClick`

→ onFocus

Table 2.54 lists the properties supported by the Reset object.

Property	NS	MS-IE	JavaScript	read only	static
form	2.0	3.0	1.0	X	
name	2.0	3.0	1.0		
type	3.0	4.0	1.1	X	
value	2.0	3.0	1.0	X	

Table 2.54 *The properties of the* Reset *object*

Table 2.55 lists the supported methods.

Method	NS	JavaScript	static
blur	2.0	1.0	
click	2.0	1.0	
focus	2.0	1.0	
handleEvent	4.0	1.2	

Table 2.55 *The methods of the* Reset *object*

Reset also inherits the watch and unwatch methods from the Object object.

See also: Button, Form, Form.onReset, onReset, Submit

blur()

The blur method removes the focus from an object.

Syntax:

```
Object.blur()
```

where Object stands for a Reset object.

See also: Reset.focus

click()

click simulates a mouse click on the Reset object. click does NOT activate the onClick event handler.

Syntax:

```
Object.click()
```

where Object stands for a Reset object.

focus()

The `focus` method sets the focus on a `Reset` object.

See also: `Reset.blur`

form

You can use this property to find out which form contains the `Reset` object.

See also: `Form`

handleEvent()

This method allows you to execute specific events.

Syntax:

`handleEvent(event)`

where `event` stands for the event to be executed.

name

The name of the `Reset` object.

type

Indicates the type of `Reset` object.

value

The value of the `Reset` object. This contains the value specified in `value` immediately after the page has been loaded.

2.1.39 screen

The `screen` object contains all the key information you need to find out the screen resolution used by the user or the number of colors the user's system can display.

This object was implemented in JavaScript 1.2.

Table 2.56 lists the properties supported by the `screen` object.

Property	NS	JavaScript	read only	static
availHeight	4.0	1.2		
availLeft	4.0	1.2		
availTop	4.0	1.2		
availWidth	4.0	1.2		
colorDepth	4.0	1.2		
height	4.0	1.2		
pixelDepth	4.0	1.2		
width	4.0	1.2		

Table 2.56 *The properties of the* `screen` *object*

The `screen` object inherits the `watch` and `unwatch` methods from the `Object` object.

availHeight

The usable height of the screen in pixels. Any taskbars, etc. that are displayed are already deducted from this property.

availLeft

The first available horizontal pixel.

availTop

The first available vertical pixel.

availWidth

The usable width of the screen in pixels. Any taskbars, etc. that are displayed are already deducted from this property.

colorDepth

The color depth in bits of the color palette used in the browser on the user's system.

height

The height of the screen in pixels.

pixelDepth

The color depth in bits used on the user's system.

width

The width of the screen in pixels.

2.1.40   Select

The Select object contains all the key information the browser needs to display option lists for a form.

This object was implemented in JavaScript 1.0.

A Select object is created by the <INPUT TYPE="SELECT"> tag in HTML.

The Select object was expanded to include the type property in version 1.1.

With effect from JavaScript version 1.2, the Select object also includes the handleEvents method.

Supported event handlers:

→ onBlur
→ onChange
→ onFocus

Table 2.57 lists the properties supported by the Select object.

Property	NS	JavaScript	read only	static
form	2.0	1.0	X	
length	2.0	1.0	X	
name	2.0	1.0		
options	2.0	1.0	X	
selectedIndex	2.0	1.0		
type	3.0	1.1	X	

Table 2.57   *The properties of the* Select *object*

Table 2.58 lists the methods supported.

Method	NS	JavaScript	static
blur	2.0	1.0	
focus	2.0	1.0	
handleEvent	4.0	1.2	

Table 2.58   *The methods of the* Select *object*

Select also inherits the watch and unwatch methods from the Object object.

See also: Form, Radio

blur()

The `blur` method removes the focus from an object.

Syntax:

`Object.blur()`

where `Object` stands for a `Select` object.

See also: `Select.focus`

focus()

The `focus` method sets the focus on a `Select` object.

See also: `Select.blur`

form

You can use this property to find out which form contains the `Select` object.

See also: `Form`

handleEvent()

You can use this method to execute specific events.

Syntax:

`handleEvent(event)`

where `event` stands for the event to be executed.

length

The number of elements in the options list.

name

The name of the `Select` object.

options

An array containing the various elements of the options list.

selectedIndex

The number of the selected element.

type

Indicates the type of `Select` object.

2.1.41 String

The `String` object contains all the key information JavaScript needs to be able to work with strings.

This object was implemented in JavaScript 1.0.

A `String` object is created by its constructor.

Syntax:

```
new String(textOfString)
```

The `String` object was expanded as follows in version 1.1:

The `prototype` property and `split` method have been added.

With effect from JavaScript version 1.2, the `String` object also includes the `concat`, `match`, `replace`, `search`, `slice` and `substr` methods.

With effect from JavaScript version 1.3, the `toSource` method was also implemented for the `String` object.

Table 2.59 lists the properties supported by the `String` object.

Property	NS	JavaScript	read only	static
constructor	3.0	1.1		
length	2.0	1.0	X	
prototype	3.0	1.1		

Table 2.59 **The properties of the** `String` **object**

Table 2.60 lists the methods supported.

Method	NS	JavaScript	static
anchor	2.0	1.0	
big	2.0	1.0	
blink	2.0	1.0	
bold	2.0	1.0	
charAt	2.0	1.0	
charCodeAt	4.0	1.2	
concat	4.0	1.2	
fixed	2.0	1.0	
fontcolor	2.0	1.0	
fontsize	2.0	1.0	
fromCharCode	4.0	1.2	X
indexOf	2.0	1.0	
italics	2.0	1.0	

Method	NS	JavaScript	static
lastIndexOf	2.0	1.0	
link	2.0	1.0	
match	4.0	1.2	
replace	4.0	1.2	
search	4.0	1.2	
slice	2.0	1.0	
small	2.0	1.0	
split	3.0	1.1	
strike	2.0	1.0	
sub	2.0	1.0	
substr	2.0	1.0	
substring	2.0	1.0	
sup	2.0	1.0	
toLowerCase	2.0	1.0	
toSource	4.06	1.3	
toString	3.0	1.1	
toUpperCase	2.0	1.0	
valueOf	3.0	1.1	

Table 2.60 *The methods of the* `String` *object*

`String` also inherits the `watch` and `unwatch` methods from the `Object` object.

anchor()

This creates an anchor.

Example:

```
document.write(text.anchor("This is an anchor"))
```

See also: `Anchor`

big()

This displays the string in enlarged characters.

blink()

This displays the string in blinking characters.

bold()

This displays the string in bold characters.

charAt()

Returns the character located at the specified position of the `String` object.

charCodeAt()

This returns the ISO Latin-1 code of the character located at the specified position of the `String` object. The first 128 characters (0-127) correspond to the ASCII code.

concat()

Appends the supplied string to the current `String` object and returns the newly created complete string.

constructor

The `constructor` property contains a direct reference to the function that creates the prototype of this object. `constructor` conforms to the ECMA-262 standard.

See also: `Object.constructor`

fixed()

This displays the string in a fixed space font.

fontcolor()

The color of the string.

fontsize()

The size of the string.

fromCharCode()

This returns a string containing the characters supplied to the method as ISO Latin-1 code. If there are several characters, these must be separated by commas.

indexOf()

This returns the position at which a supplied sequence of characters was found in the string.

Syntax:

```
indexOf(sequence[, startPosition])
```

italics()

This displays a string in italics.

lastIndexOf()

Returns the position at which a supplied sequence of characters was found in the string for the last time.

Syntax:

`lastIndexOf(sequence[, startPosition])`

length

The length of the sequence of characters.

link()

Turns a string into a hyperlink referring to the entered URL.

Syntax:

`link(URL)`

match()

Searches for the supplied regular expression in the current `String` object.

Syntax:

`match(regular expression)`

If this method meets with success, then the `RegExp` object is also altered.

prototype

The `prototype` property represents the generating function of the object that allows more properties and methods to be added to the defined object. `prototype` conforms to the ECMA-262 standard.

See also: `Function.prototype`

replace()

This replaces the place in the string found by the regular expression entered with the new string entered.

Syntax:

`replace(regularExpression, newString)`

search()

This searches for the regular expression submitted to the method. If no match is found, the method returns the value `-1`.

slice()

This returns the substring of the current `String` object. If only one number is submitted, then the result contains the complete string to the right of the value specified. If two numbers are submitted, then the substring between the two numbers is returned.

small()

Displays the string in a smaller font.

split()

This splits a string into several strings. The split is made at the positions where the submitted character was found. An array is returned containing all substrings. With effect from Netscape Communicator 4.x, the submitted character can also be a regular expression.

strike()

Displays the string in strikethrough form.

sub()

Displays the string as subscript.

substr()

This returns a substring of the current `String` object. The first number submitted indicates the position at which the substring is to start. The second number indicates the number of characters the substring is to contain.

substring()

This returns a substring of the current `String` object. If only one number is submitted, then the result contains the complete string to the right of the value specified. If two numbers are submitted, then the substring between the two numbers is returned.

sup()

Displays the string as superscript.

toLowerCase()

Outputs the whole string in lowercase letters.

toSource()

toSource returns the content of the String object. This method is normally only used by JavaScript. However you can use this method to check the content of a string object while debugging.

See also: Object.toSource

toString()

The toString method returns the value of the String object as a string. toString conforms to the ECMA-262 standard.

See also: Object.toString

toUpperCase()

Outputs the whole string in uppercase letters.

valueOf()

The elementary value of the String object is converted to a sequence of characters and returned. valueOf conforms to the ECMA-262 standard.

valueOf is normally only called internally by JavaScript.

See also: Object.valueOf

2.1.42   Style

The Style object contains all the information describing an object's style sheet template.

This object was implemented in JavaScript 1.2.

A Style object is created for all the following properties or methods of the document object:

→ document.classes
→ document.contextual
→ document.ids
→ document.tags

Table 2.61 lists the properties supported by the Style object.

Property	NS	JavaScript	read only	static
align	4.0	1.2		
backgroundColor	4.0	1.2		
backgroundImage	4.0	1.2		
borderBottomWidth	4.0	1.2		

Property	NS	JavaScript	read only	static
borderColor	4.0	1.2		
borderLeftWidth	4.0	1.2		
borderRightWidth	4.0	1.2		
borderStyle	4.0	1.2		
borderTopWidth	4.0	1.2		
clear	4.0	1.2		
color	4.0	1.2		
display	4.0	1.2		
fontFamily	4.0	1.2		
fontSize	4.0	1.2		
fontStyle	4.0	1.2		
fontWeight	4.0	1.2		
lineHeight	4.0	1.2		
listStyleType	4.0	1.2		
marginBottom	4.0	1.2		
marginLeft	4.0	1.2		
marginRight	4.0	1.2		
marginTop	4.0	1.2		
paddingBottom	4.0	1.2		
paddingLeft	4.0	1.2		
paddingRight	4.0	1.2		
paddingTop	4.0	1.2		
textAlign	4.0	1.2		
textDecoration	4.0	1.2		
textIndent	4.0	1.2		
textTransform	4.0	1.2		
whiteSpace	4.0	1.2		
width	4.0	1.2		

Table 2.61 *The properties of the* `style` *object*

Table 2.62 lists the methods supported.

Method	NS	JavaScript	static
`borderWidths`	4.0	1.2	
`margins`	4.0	1.2	
`paddings`	4.0	1.2	

Table 2.62 *The methods of the* `style` *object*

`Style` also inherits the `watch` and `unwatch` methods from the `Object` object.

align

The alignment of an HTML document.

backgroundColor

The background color.

backgroundImage

The background image.

borderBottomWidth

The width of a document's lower border.

borderColor

The color of the border of the HTML element.

borderLeftWidth

The width of the left border of an HTML element.

borderRightWidth

The width of the right border of an HTML element.

borderStyle

The style of the border around an HTML element. Possible values here are:

- ➜ `none`
- ➜ `solid`
- ➜ `double`
- ➜ `inset`
- ➜ `outset`
- ➜ `groove`
- ➜ `ridge`

In order to be seen, the border must have a width greater than `0`.

borderTopWidth

The width of the upper border of an HTML element.

borderWidths

The width of all borders of an HTML element.

clear

This specifies the pages of an HTML element that allow flowing elements.

Syntax:

```
Object.clear = (left | right | both | none)
```

color

The color of the text within the object.

display

This overwrites the normal display form of the HTML element. Possible values are:

→ none
→ block
→ inline
→ list-item

fontFamily

This defines the font of the HTML element (Helvetica, Arial, etc.).

fontSize

This defines the font size of the HTML element.

Syntax:

```
Object.fontSize = {absoluteSize | relativeSize | length | percentage}
```

Possible values:

```
absoluteSize:
```

→ xx-small
→ x-small
→ small
→ medium
→ large
→ x-large
→ xx-large

```
relativeSize:
```

→ smaller
→ larger

length: a numeric value with a unit of measurement, for example 20pt.

`percentage`: a numeric value, such as 30%.

fontStyle

This defines the style of the font (normal, italic, etc.).

fontWeight

This defines the weight of the font in an HTML element.

Syntax:

```
Object.fontWeight = { absolute | relative | value }
```

In this case `Object` stands for the `Style` object.

The value for `absolute` can be `bold` or `normal`, while the value for `relative` can be `bolder` or `lighter` and `value` can have a numeric value between `100` and `900`, where `100` stands for the lightest setting and `900` for the boldest one.

lineHeight

This defines the space between two baselines.

listStyleType

This defines the style of the point for list elements.

marginBottom

This defines the space between the lower border of the HTML element and the upper border of the nearest element.

marginLeft

This defines the space between the left border of the HTML element and the right border of the nearest element.

marginRight

This defines the space between the right border of the HTML element and the left border of the nearest element.

margins

This defines the minimum space between the borders of the HTML element and the borders of the nearest elements.

marginTop

This defines the space between the top border of the HTML element and the bottom border of the nearest element.

paddingBottom

This defines the space between the bottom border of the HTML element and the content of the HTML element.

paddingLeft

This defines the space between the left border of the HTML element and the content of the HTML element.

paddingRight

This defines the space between the right border of the HTML element and the content of the HTML element.

paddings

This defines the space between the borders of the HTML element and the content of the HTML element.

paddingTop

This defines the space between the top border of the HTML element and the content of the HTML element.

textAlign

This defines the alignment of a text in the HTML element. The following values are possible:

- → left
- → right
- → center
- → justify

textDecoration

This defines special effects for text displayed in HTML elements.

textIndent

This defines the indentation of a text in an HTML element.

textTransform

This allows you to transform text in an HTML element completely into uppercase or lowercase letters.

whiteSpace

This removes blanks before the text in the HTML element.

width

The width of the object.

2.1.43   Submit

The `Submit` object stands for a submit button in a form on a website.

This object was implemented in JavaScript 1.0.

A `Submit` object is created by the `<INPUT TYPE="SUBMIT">` tag in HTML.

In version 1.1 the `Submit` object was expanded to include the following:

The `type` property and the `blur` and `focus` methods have been added. In addition, the `onBlur` and `onFocus` event handlers have been introduced.

With effect from JavaScript version 1.2, the `Submit` object also includes the `handleEvent` method.

Supported event handlers:

→ `onBlur`
→ `onClick`
→ `onFocus`

Table 2.63 lists the properties supported by the `Submit` object.

Property	NS	JavaScript	read only	static
form	2.0	1.0	X	
name	2.0	1.0		
type	3.0	1.1	X	
value	2.0	1.0	X	

Table 2.63   *The properties of the* `Submit` *object*

Table 2.64 lists the supported methods.

Method	NS	JavaScript	static
blur	2.0	1.0	
click	2.0	1.0	
focus	2.0	1.0	
handleEvent	4.0	1.2	

Table 2.64   *The methods of the* `Submit` *object*

`Submit` also inherits the `watch` and `unwatch` methods from the `Object` object.

See also: `Button`, `Form`, `Form.onReset`, `onReset`, `Reset`

blur()

The blur method removes the focus from an object.

Syntax:

Object.blur()

where Object stands for a Submit object.

See also: Submit.focus

click()

click simulates a mouse click on the Submit object. click does NOT activate the onClick event handler.

Syntax:

Object.click()

where Object stands for a Submit object.

focus()

The focus method sets the focus on a Submit object.

See also: Submit.blur

form

You can use this property to check which form contains the Submit object.

See also: Form

handleEvent()

You can use this method to execute specific events.

Syntax:

handleEvent(event)

where event stands for the event to be executed.

name

The name of the Submit object.

type

This returns the type of Submit object.

value

The value of the `Submit` object. The value specified in `value` will be contained here directly after the page is loaded.

2.1.44 sun

A top-level object required in order to be able to use Java classes in the `sun.*` package.

This object was implemented in core JavaScript 1.1.

You do not need to create the `sun` object separately because it is predefined. You can use it without first having to call a constructor or a method.

See also: `Packages`, `Packages.sun`

2.1.45 Text

The `Text` object stands for a one-line input field in a form on a website.

This object was implemented in JavaScript 1.0.

A `Text` object is created by the `<INPUT TYPE="TEXT">` tag in HTML.

In version 1.1 the `Text` object was expanded to include the `type` property.

With effect from JavaScript version 1.2, the `Text` object also includes the `handleEvent` method.

Supported event handlers:

→ `onBlur`
→ `onChange`
→ `onFocus`
→ `onSelect`

Table 2.65 lists the properties supported by the `Text` object.

Property	NS	JavaScript	read only	static
defaultValue	2.0	1.0		
form	2.0	1.0	X	
name	2.0	1.0		
type	3.0	1.1	X	
value	2.0	1.0		

Table 2.65 *The properties of the* `Text` *object*

Table 2.66 lists the supported methods.

Method	NS	JavaScript	static
blur	2.0	1.0	
focus	2.0	1.0	
handleEvent	4.0	1.2	
select	2.0	1.0	

Table 2.66 *The methods of the* Text *object*

Text also inherits the watch and unwatch methods from the Object object.

See also: Text, Form, Password, String, Textarea

blur()

The blur method removes the focus from an object.

Syntax:

Object.blur()

where Object stands for a Text object.

See also: Text.focus

defaultValue

The default value of the Text object when created.

focus()

The focus method sets the focus on a Text object.

See also: Text.blur

form

You can use this property to check which form contains the Text object.

See also: Form

handleEvent()

You can use this method to execute specific events.

Syntax:

handleEvent(event)

where event stands for the event to be executed.

name

The name of the Text object.

select

This selects the text entered in a Text object.

See also: Text.blur, Text.focus

type

This indicates the type of the Text object.

value

The value of the Text object. The value specified in value will be contained here directly after the page is loaded.

2.1.46   Textarea

The Textarea object stands for a multi-line input field in a form on a website.

This object was implemented in JavaScript 1.0.

A Text object is created by the <INPUT TYPE="TEXTAREA"> tag in HTML.

In version 1.1 the Textarea object was expanded to include the type property.

With effect from JavaScript version 1.2, the Textarea object also includes the handleEvent method.

Supported event handlers:

→ onBlur
→ onChange
→ onFocus
→ onKeyDown
→ onKeyPress
→ onKeyUp
→ onSelect

Table 2.67 lists the properties supported by the Textarea object.

Property	NS	JavaScript	read only	static
defaultValue	2.0	1.0		
form	2.0	1.0	X	
name	2.0	1.0		
type	3.0	1.1	X	
value	2.0	1.0		

Table 2.67 *The properties of the* Textarea *object*

Table 2.68 lists the methods supported.

Method	NS	JavaScript	static
blur	2.0	1.0	
focus	2.0	1.0	
handleEvent	4.0	1.2	
select	2.0	1.0	

Table 2.68 *The methods of the* Textarea *object*

Textarea also inherits the watch and unwatch methods from the Object object.

See also: Text, Form, Password, String, Text

blur()

The blur method removes the focus from an object.

Syntax:

Object.blur()

where Object stands for a Textarea object.

See also: Textarea.focus

defaultValue

The default value the Textarea object is to have when created.

focus()

The focus method sets the focus on a Textarea object.

See also: Textarea.blur

form

You can use this property to find out which form contains the `Textarea` object.

See also: `Form`

handleEvent()

You can use this method to execute specific events.

Syntax:

`handleEvent(event)`

where `event` stands for the event to be executed.

name

The name of the `Textarea` object.

select

This selects the text entered in a `Textarea` object.

See also: `Textarea.blur`, `Textarea.focus`

type

This indicates the `Textarea` object type.

value

The value of the `Textarea` object. The value specified in `value` will be contained here immediately after the page is loaded.

2.1.47 window

The `window` object is a top-level object and represents a window or frame in a browser.

This object was implemented in JavaScript 1.0.

`window` objects are automatically created for every `<BODY>` and `<FRAMESET>` tag.

The `window` object was expanded to include the following in version 1.1:

The `closed`, `history` and `opener` are new. In addition the `blur`, `focus` and `scroll` methods and the `onBlur`, `onError` and `onFocus` event handlers were implemented in this version.

With effect from JavaScript version 1.2, the `document` object also includes the `crypto`, `innerHeight`, `innerWidth`, `locationbar`, `menubar`, `offscreen-Buffering`, `outerHeight`, `outerWidth`, `pageXOffset`, `pageYOffset`, personalbar, screenX, screenY, scrollbars, statusbar and toolbar properties. The atob, back, btoa, captureEvents, clearInterval, crypto, random, enableExternalCapture, find, forward, handle-Event, home, moveBy, moveTo, releaseEvents, resizeBy, resizeTo, routeEvent, scrollBy, scrollTo, setHotKeys, setInterval, setRe-sizable, setZOptions and stop methods were also added.

Supported event handlers:

→ onBlur
→ onDragDrop
→ onError
→ onFocus
→ onLoad
→ onMove
→ onResize
→ onUnload

Table 2.69 lists the properties supported by the window object.

Property	NS	JavaScript	read only	static
closed	3.0	1.1	X	
crypto	4.0	1.2	X	
defaultStatus	2.0	1.0		
document	2.0	1.0		
frames	2.0	1.0	X	
history	3.0	1.1		
innerHeight	4.0	1.2		
innerWidth	4.0	1.2		
length	2.0	1.0	X	
location	2.0	1.0		
locationbar	4.0	1.2		
menubar	4.0	1.2		
name	2.0	1.0		
offscreenBuffering	4.0	1.2		
opener	3.0	1.1		
outerHeight	4.0	1.2		
outerWidth	4.0	1.2		
pageXOffset	4.0	1.2	X	
pageYOffset	4.0	1.2	X	
parent	2.0	1.0	X	
personalbar	4.0	1.2		

Property	NS	JavaScript	read only	static
screenX	4.0	1.2		
screenY	4.0	1.2		
scrollbars	4.0	1.2		
self	2.0	1.0	X	
status	2.0	1.0		
statusbar	4.0	1.2		
toolbar	4.0	1.2		
top	2.0	1.0	X	
window	2.0	1.0	X	

Table 2.69 *The properties of the* `window` *object*

Table 2.70 lists the supported methods.

Method	NS	JavaScript	static
alert	2.0	1.0	
atob	4.0	1.2	
back	4.0	1.2	
blur	2.0	1.0	
btoa	4.0	1.2	
captureEvents	4.0	1.2	
clearInterval	4.0	1.2	
clearTimeout	2.0	1.0	
close	2.0	1.0	
confirm	2.0	1.0	
crypto.random	4.0	1.2	X
crypto.signText	4.0	1.2	X
disableExternalCapture	4.0	1.2	
enableExternalCapture	4.0	1.2	
find	4.0	1.2	
focus	3.0	1.1	
forward	4.0	1.2	
handleEvent	4.0	1.2	
home	4.0	1.2	
moveBy	4.0	1.2	
moveTo	4.0	1.2	
open	2.0	1.0	
print	4.0	1.2	
promt	2.0	1.0	
releaseEvents	4.0	1.2	

Method	NS	JavaScript	static
resizeBy	4.0	1.2	
resizeTo	4.0	1.2	
routeEvent	4.0	1.2	
scroll	3.0	1.1	
scrollBy	4.0	1.2	
scrollTo	4.0	1.2	
setHotKeys	4.0	1.2	
setInterval	4.0	1.2	
setResizable	4.0	1.2	
setTimeout	2.0	1.0	
setZOptions	4.0	1.2	
stop	4.0	1.2	

Table 2.70 *The methods of the* `window` *object*

`window` also inherits the `watch` and `unwatch` methods from the `Object` object.

See also: `document`, `Frame`

alert()

This opens a popup window and displays the submitted text in it.

atob()

This decodes data encoded in base 64 format.

back()

This goes one step back in the history list.

blur()

The `blur` method removes the focus from an object.

Syntax:

```
Object.blur()
```

where `Object` stands for a `window` object.

See also: `window.focus`

btoa()

This encodes binary data in base 64 format.

captureEvents()

`captureEvents` captures events as they arise and transfers them to the `window` object.

Syntax:

`captureEvents(event)`

If you want to capture several events, then these must be separated using OR characters (`|`).

clearInterval()

This clears an interval timer started with `setInterval()`.

clearTimeout()

This clears a timer set with `setTimeout()`.

close()

This closes the window. If this is a window that was not created with JavaScript, then the user is asked whether the window may be closed. If the `window` object represents a frame, then the `close()` method has no effect.

closed

Indicates whether a window is closed, i.e. minimized.

confirm()

This opens a window displaying the submitted text. The user can press an OK or CANCEL button in this window. If he presses OK, then the method returns the value `true`.

crypto

The `crypto` object, used to access the browser's encryption mechanisms.

crypto.random()

Returns a random string with a length corresponding to the submitted value.

crypto.signText()

Returns the submitted text in encrypted form.

defaultStatus

The default message displayed in the status line.

disableExternalCapture()

This terminates external event capturing as set by the `enableExternalCapture()` method.

document

This contains information about the current document and provides methods for displaying the document to the user.

enableExternalCapture()

This allows the `window` object to react to events that occur in other windows or frames opened by this `window` object.

find()

This searches the current window for a submitted string.

focus()

The `focus` method sets the focus on a `window` object.

See also: `window.blur`

forward()

Moves one step forward in the history list.

frames

Array containing the `Frame` objects controlled by this page. The sequence reflects the order of appearance of the `<FRAME>` tags in the source code.

handleEvent()

You can use this method to execute specific events.

Syntax:

`handleEvent(event)`

where `event` stands for the event to be executed.

history

This contains information about URLs this `window` object has already visited.

home()

This allows the browser to change to the browser welcome page defined in the settings.

innerHeight

The usable height of the browser window in pixels.

innerWidth

The usable width of the browser window in pixels.

length

This indicates the number of frames in a window.

location

This contains information about the current URL.

locationbar

This represents the browser location bar.

menubar

The browser menu bar.

moveBy()

Moves the window by the specified number of pixels relative to its current position.

Syntax:

```
moveBy(horizontal, vertical)
```

moveTo()

Moves the top left corner of the window to the specified position on the screen.

Syntax:

```
moveTo(x, y)
```

name

The name of the `window` object.

offscreenBuffering

Defines whether the window refresh is first to take place in an offscreen buffer.

open()

Opens a new browser window.

Syntax:

```
open(URL, windowName[, windowAttribute])
```

URL stands for the URL to be opened. windowName specifies the name of the new window and windowAttribute can contain several values from the following table separated by commas.

windowAttribute	Description
alwaysLowered=yes|no	Always keep the window in the background (yes/no). This attribute requires signed scripts.
alwaysRaised=yes|no	Always keep the window in the foreground (yes/no). This attribute requires signed scripts.
dependent=yes|no	The window closes when the calling window is closed. (yes/no)
directories=yes|no	Display the standard directory buttons in the browser (on/off). For example *What's new?*
height=pixel	Height in pixels.
hotkeys=yes|no	Enable hotkeys (yes/no).
innerHeight=pixel	Height of the usable area in pixels.
innerWidth=pixel	Width of the usable area in pixels.
location=yes|no	Display the URL (on/off).
menubar=yes|no	Menu bar (on/off).
outerHeight=pixel	The height of the browser window in pixels. This attribute requires signed scripts.
outerWidth=pixel	The width of the browser window in pixels. This attribute requires signed scripts.
personalbar=yes|no	Bookmark bar (yes/no).
resizable=yes|no	Is the user permitted to change the size of the window? (yes/no)
screenX=pixel	The x position of the window in pixels. This attribute requires signed scripts.
screenY=pixel	The y position of the window in pixels. This attribute requires signed scripts.
scrollbars=yes|no	Scrollbars (on/off).
status=yes|no	Status bar (on/off).
titlebar=yes|no	Window border and title bar (on/off). This attribute requires signed scripts.
toolbar=yes|no	Toolbar (on/off).
width=pixel	Width in pixels.

windowAttribute	Description
z-lock=yes|no	The window does not enter the foreground when activated (yes/no). This attribute requires signed scripts.

opener

This contains a link to the window containing the calling document.

outerHeight

This contains the outer height of the window in pixels.

outerWidth

This contains the outer width of the window in pixels.

pageXOffset

This specifies the x position of the top left corner of the window currently displayed in pixels.

pageYOffset

This specifies the y position of the top left corner of the window currently displayed in pixels.

parent

The `window` object containing the currently displayed window or frame.

personalbar

Specifies whether or not the bookmark location bar is to be displayed.

print()

Prints the contents of the window.

prompt()

This shows the user an input dialog.

releaseEvents()

`releaseEvents` halts the capture of events that arise.

Syntax:

```
releaseEvents(event)
```

If you wish to halt the capture of several events, then these must be separated by OR characters (|).

resizeBy()

This shifts the bottom right corner of the window inwards by the specified x and y values.

resizeTo()

This resets the height and width of a window to the specified values.

routeEvent()

This routes captured events to the normal events hierarchy.

screenX

The x value of the left side of a window.

screenY

The y value of the top side of a window.

scroll()

Scrolls the content of the window to the specified position.

Tip With effect from JavaScript 1.2, this method is replaced by the scrollTo method. However it is still implemented for reasons of compatibility.

scrollbars

This represents the window scrollbar.

scrollBy()

This scrolls the content of the window horizontally and vertically by the specified number of pixels.

scrollTo()

This scrolls the content of the window to the specified position.

self

This points to the calling `window` object.

setHotKeys

This activates or deactivates hotkeys in windows with no menus.

setInterval()

This sets a timer after which a function or command is always executed.

Syntax:

```
setInterval(command, milliseconds)
setInterval(function, milliseconds [, argument1[, ...,
argumentN]])
```

setResizable()

This specifies whether the user is permitted to change the size of the window.

setTimeout

This sets a timer after which a function or command is executed once.

Syntax:

```
setTimeout(command, milliseconds)
setTimeout(function, milliseconds [, argument1[, ..., argu-
mentN]])
```

setZOptions()

This indicates a window's z-order cascading setting.

status

This sets the value of the status bar.

statusbar

This refers to the browser status bar.

stop

This stops all loading in the current window.

toolbar

This represents the browser toolbar.

top

This refers to the topmost window displayed on the screen.

window

This refers to the window or frame currently under use.

2.2 Top-level properties and functions

This section deals with properties and functions that are not assigned to objects. Table 2.71 contains an overview of top-level properties in JavaScript.

Property	NS	JavaScript	read only	static
Infinity	4.06	1.3		
NaN	4.06	1.3		
undefined	4.06	1.3		

Table 2.71 *Top-level properties of JavaScript*

Table 2.72 contains an overview of the top-level functions of JavaScript.

Function	NS	JavaScript	static
escape	2.0	1.0	
eval	2.0	1.0	
isFinite	4.06	1.3	
isNaN	2.0	1.0	
Number	4.0	1.2	
parseFloat	2.0	1.0	
parseInt	2.0	1.0	
String	4.0	1.2	
taint	3.0	1.1	
unescape	2.0	1.0	
untaint	3.0	1.1	

Table 2.72 *Top-level functions of JavaScript*

All of the properties and functions listed above comply with the ECMA-262 standard.

2.2.1   escape()

escape() returns a string which has been encoded suitable for use in form data.

This function was implemented in core JavaScript 1.0.

Syntax:

```
escape("string")
```

Example:

```
escape("Drag&Drop is a great feature.")
```

Returns the following string:

```
"Drag%26Drop%20is%20a%20great%20feature."
```

See also: unescape().

2.2.2   eval()

eval() evaluates the specified string as JavaScript and returns the result.

This function was implemented in core JavaScript 1.0.

Syntax:

```
eval(string)
```

Example 1:

```
eval(new String("This is a string."))
```

Returns the following result:

```
This is a string.
```

Example 2:

```
eval("25+13")
```

Returns the following result:

```
38
```

See also: Object.eval().

2.2.3   Infinity

Infinity represents an infinite numerical value.

This property was implemented in core JavaScript 1.3.

Syntax:

```
Infinity
```

See also:

`Number.NEGATIVE_INFINITY, Number.POSITIVE_INFINITY.`

2.2.4   isFinite()

`isFinite()` checks a specified number to ensure it is finite.

This function was implemented in core JavaScript 1.3.

Syntax:

`isFinite(number)`

2.2.5   isNaN()

`isNaN()` checks whether or not the value specified is a number. This method returns the value `true` if the tested value is not a number.

This function was implemented in core JavaScript 1.0 but was only available for UNIX. With effect from core JavaScript 1.1, `isNaN()` is available on all platforms.

Syntax:

`isNaN(value)`

Example:

```
if (isNaN(value)) {
   notANumber()
} else {
   isANumber()
}
```

This example checks whether the variable `value` is a number. If `value` is not a number, then the `notANumber` function is called. If `value` is a number, then `isANumber` function is called.

2.2.6   NaN

A special value that indicates that an arithmetical expression has returned a value that is not a number.

This property was implemented in JavaScript 1.3.

2.2.7 Number()

This converts the specified object into a number.

This function was implemented in JavaScript 1.2.

Syntax:

```
Number(object)
```

Example:

```
date = new Date("July 21, 2000 10:00:00")
alert (Number(date))
```

These statements would result in the window shown in Figure 2.7.

Figure 2.7 *The output from the top-level* Number() *function*

2.2.8 parseFloat()

This transforms a string into a floating decimal number.

This function was implemented in JavaScript 1.0.

Syntax:

```
parseFloat(string)
```

Example 1:

```
parseFloat("21.567")
parseFloat("21567e-3")
parseFloat("0.21567E+2")
```

All statements return the floating point number 21.567.

Example 2:

```
parseFloat("Test")
```

Returns the result NaN.

2.2.9   parseInt()

This transforms a string into an integer.

This function was implemented in JavaScript 1.0.

Syntax:

```
parseInt(string[, base])
```

Example:

```
parseInt("F", 16)
parseInt("17", 8)
parseInt("15.99", 10)
parseInt("15", 10)
```

All of the examples above return the number 15. If a string that cannot be transformed is specified, the function returns NaN.

2.2.10   String()

Converts the specified object into a string.

This function was implemented in JavaScript 1.2.

Syntax:

```
String(object)
```

Example:

```
date = new Date(964166400000)
alert (String(date))
```

Figure 2.8 shows the window that would appear as a result of these statements.

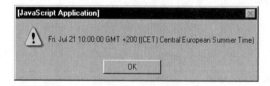

[JavaScript Application]

Fri. Jul 21 10:00:00 GMT +200 [(CET) Central European Summer Time]

OK

Figure 2.8 *Output of the top-level function* String()

2.2.11   taint()

Taints data to indicate unreliable content.

This function was implemented in JavaScript 1.1.

Syntax:

```
taint([nameOfDataElement])
```

2.2.12   undefined

A special value which indicates that this value is not defined.

This property was implemented in JavaScript 1.3.

2.2.13   unescape()

Transforms all characters in the specified string into normal ASCII characters and returns the resulting string. The string that is specified must contain a percentage symbol for each character to be transformed (%) as well as the hexadecimal value for the character from the ASCII character table.

This function was implemented in JavaScript 1.0.

Syntax:

```
unescape(string)
```

2.2.14   untaint()

Marks previously tainted data as clean.

This function was implemented in JavaScript 1.1.

Syntax:

```
untaint([nameOfDataElement])
```

2.3 Event handlers

This section contains all the information you will need to use event handlers.

Event	Event handler	Description
Abort	onAbort	Executes JavaScript code if the user aborts an action.
Blur	onBlur	Executes JavaScript code when an element in a form, window or frame loses focus.
Change	onChange	Executes JavaScript code when a Select, Text or Textarea input field loses focus and has its data changed.
Click	onClick	Executes JavaScript code when the user clicks on an element in a form.
DblClick	onDblClick	Executes JavaScript code when the user double-clicks on an element in a form.
DragDrop	onDragDrop	Executes JavaScript code when the user drags an object (a file, etc.) into the browser window and drops it there.
Error	onError	Executes JavaScript code when an error occurs while a document or image is loading.
Focus	onFocus	Executes JavaScript code when an element is assigned focus.
KeyDown	onKeyDown	Executes JavaScript code when the user presses down a key on the keyboard.
KeyPress	onKeyPress	Executes JavaScript code when the user presses or holds down a key on the keyboard.
KeyUp	onKeyUp	Executes JavaScript code when the user releases a key on the keyboard.
Load	onLoad	Executes JavaScript code when the browser has finished loading a document or all the frames contained in a `<FRAMESET>` tag.
MouseDown	onMouseDown	Executes JavaScript code when the user presses a mouse key.
MouseMove	onMouseMove	Executes JavaScript code when the user moves the mouse.
MouseOut	onMouseOut	Executes JavaScript code when the mouse cursor quits an area (image or link). The mouse cursor must have been inside the area prior to this.

Event	Event handler	Description
MouseOver	onMouseOver	Executes JavaScript code when the mouse cursor is moved into an area (image or link). The mouse cursor must have been outside the area prior to this.
MouseUp	onMouseUp	Executes JavaScript code when the user releases the mouse button.
Move	onMove	Executes JavaScript code when the user or a script moves a window or a frame.
Reset	onReset	Executes JavaScript code when the user resets a form.
Resize	onResize	Executes JavaScript code when the user or a script alters the size of a window or frame.
Select	onSelect	Executes JavaScript code when the user selects an area in a Text or Textarea field.
Submit	onSubmit	Executes JavaScript code when a user submits a form.
Unload	onUnload	Executes JavaScript code when a user quits a document.

Table 2.73 *Client-side JavaScript event handlers*

There follows a list describing the syntax and any properties of the event handlers mentioned above.

2.3.1   onAbort

`onAbort` executes JavaScript code when the user aborts an action.

Property	Description
type	The event type.
target	Refers to the object to which this event was originally sent.

Table 2.74 *The properties of* `onAbort`

2.3.2   onBlur

`onBlur` executes JavaScript code when an element of a form, window or frame loses focus.

Property	Description
type	The event type.
target	Refers to the object to which this event was originally sent.

Table 2.75 *The properties of* `onBlur`

2.3.3 onChange

onChange executes JavaScript code when a Select, Text or Textarea input field loses focus and when its data has been altered.

Property	Description
type	The event type.
target	Refers to the object to which this event was originally sent.

Table 2.76 *The properties of* onChange

2.3.4 onClick

onClick executes JavaScript code when you click on an element in a form.

Property	Description
type	The event type.
target	Refers to the object to which this event was originally sent.
layerX, layerY, pageX, pageY, screenX, screenY	The position of the cursor when the event was activated.
which	which contains the values 1 and 3 with the left and right mouse buttons respectively.
modifiers	This contains an array with the keys pressed while mouse button was pressed.

Table 2.77 *The properties of* onClick

2.3.5 onDblClick

onDblClick executes JavaScript code when you double-click on an element in a form.

Property	Description
type	The event type.
target	Refers to the object to which this event was originally sent.
layerX, layerY, pageX, pageY, screenX, screenY	The position of the cursor when the event was activated.
which	which contains the values 1 and 3 with the left and right mouse buttons respectively.
modifiers	This contains an array with the keys pressed while mouse button was pressed.

Table 2.78 *The properties of* onDblClick

2.3.6   onDragDrop

`onDragDrop` executes JavaScript code when the user drags an object (a file, etc.) into the browser window and drops it there.

Property	Description
type	The event type.
target	Refers to the object to which this event was originally sent.
data	Contains an array with the URLs of the objects that have been inserted.
modifiers	This contains an array with the pressed keys while the key was pressed.
screenX, screenY	The position of the cursor when the event was activated.

Table 2.79   *The properties of* `onDragDrop`

2.3.7   onError

`onError` executes JavaScript code when an error occurs while a document or image is being loaded.

Property	Description
type	The event type.
target	Refers to the object to which this event was originally sent.

Table 2.80   *The properties of* `onError`

2.3.8   onFocus

`onFocus` executes JavaScript code when an element loses focus.

Property	Description
type	The event type.
target	Refers to the object to which this event was originally sent.

Table 2.81   *The properties of* `onFocus`

2.3.9   onKeyDown

`onKeyDown` executes JavaScript code when a key on the keyboard is pressed down.

Property	Description
type	The event type.
target	Refers to the object to which this event was originally sent.
layerX, layerY, pageX, pageY, screenX, screenY	The position of the cursor when the event was activated.
which	Contains the ASCII code of the key that was pressed.
modifiers	Contains an array with the keys pressed while the key was held down.

Table 2.82   *The properties of* `onKeyDown`

2.3.10   onKeyPress

`onKeyPress` executes JavaScript code when the user presses a key or holds it down.

Property	Description
type	The event type.
target	Refers to the object to which this event was originally sent.
layerX, layerY, pageX, pageY, screenX, screenY	The position of the cursor when the event was activated.
which	Contains the ASCII code of the key that was pressed.
modifiers	Contains an array with the keys pressed while the key was held down.

Table 2.83   *The properties of* `onKeyPress`

2.3.11   onKeyUp

`onKeyUp` executes JavaScript code when a key on the keyboard is released again.

Property	Description
type	The event type.
target	Refers to the object to which this event was originally sent.
layerX, layerY, pageX, pageY, screenX, screenY	The position of the cursor when the event was activated.

Property	Description
which	Contains the ASCII code of the key that was pressed.
modifiers	Contains an array with the keys pressed while the key was held down.

Table 2.84 *The properties of* onKeyUp

2.3.12   onLoad

onLoad executes JavaScript code when the browser has finished loading a document or all frames contained in a <FRAMESET> tag.

Property	Description
type	The event type.
target	Refers to the object to which this event was originally sent.
width, height	The width and height of the window or frame.

Table 2.85 *The properties of* onLoad

2.3.13   onMouseDown

onMouseDown executes JavaScript code when the user presses down a mouse button.

Property	Description
type	The event type.
target	Refers to the object to which this event was originally sent.
layerX, layerY, pageX, pageY, screenX, screenY	The position of the mouse button when the event was activated.
which	which contains the values 1 and 3 for the left and right mouse buttons respectively.
modifiers	Contains an array with the keys pressed while the mouse button was held down.

Table 2.86 *The properties of* onMouseDown

2.3.14   onMouseMove

onMouseMove executes JavaScript code when the user moves the mouse.

Property	Description
type	The event type.
target	Refers to the object to which this event was originally sent.
layerX, layerY, pageX, pageY, screenX, screenY	The position of the mouse cursor when the event was activated.

Table 2.87   *The properties of* onMouseMove

2.3.15   onMouseOut

onMouseOut executes JavaScript code when the mouse cursor moves out of an area (image or link). The mouse cursor must have been inside the area prior to this.

Property	Description
type	The event type.
target	Refers to the object to which this event was originally sent.
layerX, layerY, pageX, pageY, screenX, screenY	The position of the mouse cursor when the event was activated.

Table 2.88   *The properties of* onMouseOut

2.3.16   onMouseOver

onMouseOver executes JavaScript code when the mouse cursor moves into an area (image or link). The mouse cursor must have been outside the area prior to this.

Property	Description
type	The event type.
target	Refers to the object to which this event was originally sent.
layerX, layerY, pageX, pageY, screenX, screenY	The position of the mouse cursor when the event was activated.

Table 2.89   *The properties of* onMouseOver

2.3.17   onMouseUp

onMouseUp executes JavaScript code when the user releases the mouse button.

Property	Description
type	The event type.
target	Refers to the object to which this event was originally sent.
layerX, layerY, pageX, pageY, screenX, screenY	The position of the mouse cursor when the event was activated.
which	which has the values 1 and 3 for the left and right mouse buttons respectively.
modifiers	Contains an array with the keys pressed while the mouse button was released.

Table 2.90   *The properties of* onMouseUp

2.3.18 onMove

`onMove` executes JavaScript code when the user or a script moves a window or a frame.

Property	Description
type	The event type.
target	Refers to the object to which this event was originally sent.
screenX, screenY	The top left corner of the window or frame.

Table 2.91 *The properties of* `onMove`

2.3.19 onReset

`onReset` executes JavaScript code when the user resets a form.

Property	Description
type	The event type.
target	Refers to the object to which this event was originally sent.

Table 2.92 *The properties of* `onReset`

2.3.20 onResize

`onResize` executes JavaScript code when the user or a script changes the size of a window or frame.

Property	Description
type	The event type.
target	Refers to the object to which this event was originally sent.
width, height	The width and height of the window or frame.

Table 2.93 *The properties of* `onResize`

2.3.21 onSelect

`onSelect` executes JavaScript code when the user highlights an area in a Text or Textarea field.

Property	Description
type	The event type.
target	Refers to the object to which this event was originally sent.

Table 2.94 *The properties of* `onSelect`

2.3.22   onSubmit

`onSubmit` executes JavaScript code when the user submits a form.

Property	Description
type	The event type.
target	Refers to the object to which this event was originally sent.

Table 2.95   *The properties of* `onSubmit`

2.3.23   onUnload

`onUnload` executes JavaScript code when a user quits a document.

Property	Description
type	The event type.
target	Refers to the object to which this event was originally sent.

Table 2.96   *The properties of* `onUnload`

2.4 Reserved words

Table 2.97 lists all reserved words in JavaScript.

These words may not be used for the names of variables, objects, methods and functions.

Reserved words			
abstract	else	instanceof	switch
boolean	enum	int	synchronized
break	export	interface	this
byte	extends	long	throw
case	false	native	throws
catch	final	new	transient
char	finally	null	true
class	float	package	try
const	for	private	typeof
continue	function	protected	var
debugger	goto	public	void
default	if	return	volatile
delete	implements	short	while
do	import	static	with
double	in	super	

Table 2.97 *Reserved words in JavaScript*

Part II

Go ahead!

Tips and tricks

3

This chapter contains scripts that you can use as a guideline when you start programming in JavaScript by yourself.

> **Tip** The examples in this chapter are based on examples from the http://javascript.internet.com/ website.

3.1 Cookies

The following scripts save cookies (user data) locally on the hard disk.

3.1.1 Cookie for counter

The following script creates a cookie that tells the user how often he has visited this page.

```
<SCRIPT>
function GetCookie (name) {
var arg = name + "=";
var alen = arg.length;
var clen = document.cookie.length;
var i = 0;
while (i < clen) {
var j = i + alen;
if (document.cookie.substring(i, j) == arg)
return getCookieVal (j);
i = document.cookie.indexOf(" ", i) + 1;
if (i == 0) break;
```

```
}
return null;
}
function SetCookie (name, value) {
var argv = SetCookie.arguments;
var argc = SetCookie.arguments.length;
var expires = (argc > 2) ? argv[2] : null;
var path = (argc > 3) ? argv[3] : null;
var domain = (argc > 4) ? argv[4] : null;
var secure = (argc > 5) ? argv[5] : false;
document.cookie = name + "=" + escape (value) +
((expires == null) ? "" : ("; expires="
+ expires.toGMTString())) +
((path == null) ? "" : ("; path=" + path)) +
((domain == null) ? "" : ("; domain=" + domain)) +
((secure == true) ? "; secure" : "");
}
function DeleteCookie (name) {
var exp = new Date();
exp.setTime (exp.getTime() - 1);
var cval = GetCookie (name);
document.cookie = name + "=" + cval + "; expires=" +
exp.toGMTString();
}
var expDays = 30;
var exp = new Date();
exp.setTime(exp.getTime() + (expDays*24*60*60*1000));
function amt(){
var count = GetCookie('count')
if(count == null) {
SetCookie('count','1')
return 1
}
else {
var newcount = parseInt(count) + 1;
DeleteCookie('count')
SetCookie('count',newcount,exp)
return count
}
}
function getCookieVal(offset) {
var endstr = document.cookie.indexOf (";", offset);
```

```
if (endstr == -1)
endstr = document.cookie.length;
return unescape(document.cookie.substring(offset, endstr));
}
</SCRIPT>
<SCRIPT>
document.write("You have already visited this page <b>" +
amt() + "</b> times.")
</SCRIPT>
```

3.1.2   Cookie for counter with name

The following script creates a cookie that tells the user how often he or she has
visited this page. The user's name is also stored and an indicator appears showing when the user last visited the site.

```
<HTML>
<HEAD>
<SCRIPT LANGUAGE="JavaScript">
var expDays = 30;
var exp = new Date();
exp.setTime(exp.getTime() + (expDays*24*60*60*1000));

function Who(info){
  var VisitorName = GetCookie('VisitorName')
  if (VisitorName == null) {
    VisitorName = set();
  }
  return VisitorName;
}

function When(info){
  var rightNow = new Date()
  var WWHTime = 0;
  WWHTime = GetCookie('WWhenH')
  var lastHereFormatting = new Date(WWHTime);
  var lastHereInDateFormat = "" + lastHereFormatting;
  var dayOfWeek = lastHereInDateFormat.substring(0,3)
  var dateMonth = lastHereInDateFormat.substring(4,11)
  var timeOfDay = lastHereInDateFormat.substring(11,19)
  var year = lastHereInDateFormat.substring(23,25)
  var WWHText = dayOfWeek + ", " + dateMonth + " "
    + year + " at " + timeOfDay
```

```
    SetCookie ("WWhenH", rightNow)
    return WWHText
  }
function Count(info){
  var WWHCount = GetCookie('WWHCount')
  if (isNaN(WWHCount)) WWHCount = 0;
  if (WWHCount == null) {
    WWHCount = 0;
}else{
  WWHCount++;
}
SetCookie ('WWHCount', WWHCount);
return WWHCount;
}

function set(){
  var dateNow = new Date()
  VisitorName = prompt("Who are you?");
  SetCookie ('VisitorName', VisitorName);
  SetCookie ('WWHCount', 0);
  SetCookie ('WWhenH', dateNow);
  return VisitorName
}
function getCookieVal (offset) {
  var endstr = document.cookie.indexOf (";", offset);
  if (endstr == -1)
    endstr = document.cookie.length;
  return unescape(document.cookie.substring(offset,
              endstr));
}

function GetCookie (name) {
  var arg = name + "=";
  var alen = arg.length;
  var clen = document.cookie.length;
  var i = 0;
  while (i < clen) {
    var j = i + alen;
    if (document.cookie.substring(i, j) == arg)
     return getCookieVal (j);
  i = document.cookie.indexOf(" ", i) + 1;
  if (i == 0) break;
```

```
}
  return null;
}

function SetCookie (name, value) {
  var argv = SetCookie.arguments;
  var argc = SetCookie.arguments.length;
  var expires = (argc > 2) ? argv[2] : null;
  var path = (argc > 3) ? argv[3] : null;
  var domain = (argc > 4) ? argv[4] : null;
  var secure = (argc > 5) ? argv[5] : false;
  document.cookie = name + "=" + escape (value) +
  ((expires == null) ? "" : ("; expires=" +
  expires.toGMTString())) + ((path == null) ?
  "" : ("; path=" + path)) + ((domain == null)
  ? "" : ("; domain=" + domain))
  + ((secure == true) ? "; secure" : "");
}

function DeleteCookie (name) {
  var exp = new Date();
  exp.setTime (exp.getTime() - 1);
  var cval = GetCookie (name);
  document.cookie = name + "=" + cval
    + "; expires=" + exp.toGMTString();
}
</SCRIPT>
<BODY>
<CENTER>
<SCRIPT LANGUAGE="JavaScript">
document.write("Hello " + Who() +
    ". You have already visited this page "
    + Count()
    + " times.  The date of your last visit was "
    + When() +".");
</SCRIPT>
</CENTER>
</HTML>
```

3.2 Scripts for menus

The following scripts are intended for displaying menus on Internet pages.

3.2.1 Menu via drop-down field

A selection field containing Internet pages that switches to these pages after the start button is pressed.

```
<HTML>
  <HEAD>
    <SCRIPT LANGUAGE="JavaScript">
<!—Hide for old browsers --
      function surfto(form) {
        var myindex=form.dest.selectedIndex
        location=form.dest.options[myindex].value;
      }
// End hiding -->
    </SCRIPT>
  </HEAD>
  <BODY>
  <FORM NAME="myform">
  <SELECT NAME="dest" SIZE=1>
    <OPTION SELECTED VALUE="http://www.aw.com/cseng/
">Addison-Wesley
    <OPTION VALUE="http://www.pearsoned-ema.com/">Pearson
Education
    <OPTION VALUE="http://www.ft.com/">FT.com
  </SELECT>
  <INPUT TYPE="BUTTON" VALUE="Start"
    onClick="surfto(this.form)">
  </BODY>
</HTML>
```

3.2.2 Menu via drop-down field in frames

You can improve the above menu by placing it on a frame page. You can create a frame page using the following program:

```
<HTML>
<FRAMESET ROWS=10%,90%>
  <FRAME SRC="menu2.htm" NAME="menu">
```

```
    <FRAME SRC="" NAME="display">
</FRAMESET>
</HTML>
```

The menu should then look like this and should be saved as `menu2.htm`:

```
<HTML>
  <HEAD>
    <SCRIPT LANGUAGE="JavaScript">
<!—Hide for old browsers --
function surfto(form) {
        var myindex=form.dest.selectedIndex
        window.open(form.dest.options[myindex].value,
        target="display");
}
// End hiding -->
    </SCRIPT>
  </HEAD>
  <BODY>
  <CENTER>
  <FORM NAME="myform">
  <SELECT NAME="dest" SIZE=1>
    <OPTION SELECTED VALUE="http://www.aw.com/cseng/
">Addison-Wesley
    <OPTION VALUE="http://www.pearsoned-ema.com/">Pearson
Education
    <OPTION VALUE="http://www.ft.com/">FT.com
  </SELECT>
  <INPUT TYPE="BUTTON" VALUE="Start"
    onClick="surfto(this.form)">
  </FORM>
  </CENTER>
  </BODY>
</HTML>
```

The advantage of implementing a menu in this way is that the user does not have to leave your page.

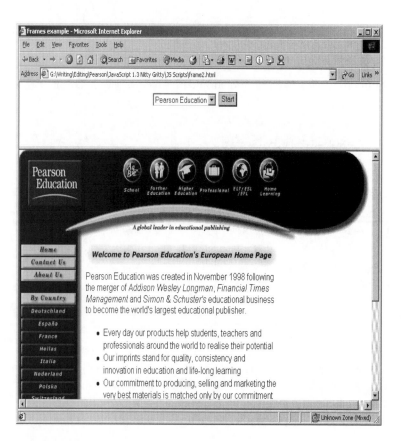

Figure 3.1   *A menu that works with frames*

3.2.3   Movable menu

You can move this menu about.

```
<HTML>
  <HEAD>
    <SCRIPT LANGUAGE="JavaScript">
    function checkVersion4() {
      var x = navigator.appVersion;
      y = x.substring(0,4);
      if (y>=4) setVariables();moveOB();
    }
      objectX="object11"
      XX=-70;
      YY=-70;
      OB=11;
```

```
function setVariables() {
  if (navigator.appName == "Netscape") {
    h=".left=";v=".top=";dS="document.";sD="";
  }
  else{
    h=".pixelLeft=";v=".pixelTop=";dS="";sD=".style";
  }
}

function setObject(a) {
  objectX="object"+a;
  OB=a;
  XX=eval("xpos"+a);
  YY=eval("ypos"+a);
}

function getObject() {
  if (isNav) document.captureEvents(Event.MOUSEMOVE);
}

function releaseObject() {
  if (isNav) document.releaseEvents(Event.MOUSEMOVE);
  check="no";
  objectX="object11";
  document.close();
}

function moveOB() {
  eval(dS + objectX + sD + h + Xpos);
  eval(dS + objectX + sD + v + Ypos);
}

var isNav = (navigator.appName.indexOf("Netscape") !=-
1);
var isIE = (navigator.appName.indexOf("Microsoft") !=-
1);
nsValue=(document.layers);
check="no";

function MoveHandler(e) {
  Xpos = (isIE) ? event.clientX : e.pageX;
```

```
      Ypos = (nsValue) ? e.pageY : event.clientY;
      if (check=="no") {
        diffX=XX-Xpos;
        diffY=YY-Ypos;
        check="yes";
        if (objectX=="object11") check="no";
      }
      Xpos+=diffX;
      Ypos+=diffY;
      if (OB=="1") xpos1=Xpos,ypos1=Ypos;
      moveOB();
    }

    if (isNav) {
      document.captureEvents(Event.CLICK);
      document.captureEvents(Event.DBLCLICK);
    }

  xpos1=50;
  ypos1=50;
  xpos11 = -50;
  ypos11 = -50;
  Xpos=5;
  Ypos=5;
  document.onmousemove = MoveHandler;
  document.onclick = getObject;
  document.ondblclick = releaseObject;
</SCRIPT>
</HEAD>


<BODY OnLoad="checkVersion4()">


<B>Click on "Move Menu" to move the menu.<BR>
Double-click to place it in another location.</B>
<BR>

<DIV ID="object1" STYLE="position:absolute;
visibility:show; left:50px; top:50px; z-index:2">
<TABLE BORDER=1 CELLPADDING=5>
<TR>
```

```
<TD BGCOLOR=EEEEEE>
<CENTER>
<A HREF="javascript:void(0)"
onmousedown="setObject(1)">Move Menu</a>
</CENTER>
</TD>
</TR>
<TR>
<TD>
  <CENTER>
  <BR>
  <A HREF="http://www.aw.com/cseng/">Addison-Wesley</A><br>
  <A HREF="http://www.pearsoned-ema.com/">Pearson Education
    </a><br>
  <A HREF="http://www.ft.com/">FT.com</a>
  </CENTER>
</TD>
</TR>
</TABLE>
</DIV>

<DIV ID="object11" STYLE="position:absolute;
visibility:show; left:-70px; top:-70px; z-index:2">
</DIV>
</HTML>
```

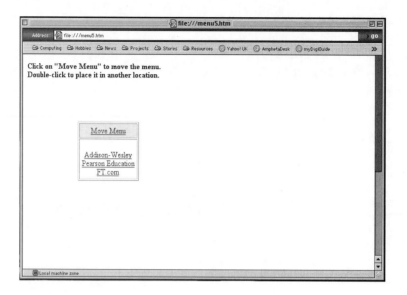

Figure 3.2 *A movable menu*

3.2.4 Menu tree

This menu works with frames. You should save the page that creates the frame
under `frame2.htm`.

```
<HTML>
<FRAMESET COLS="175,*">
    <FRAME SRC="menu.htm" NAME="menu">
    <FRAME SRC="" NAME="display">
</FRAMESET>
</HTML>
```

Next we need the menu.htm file.

```
<HTML>
<HEAD>

<STYLE TYPE="text/css">
a
{text-decoration: none;}

.title
{position: absolute;
width: 100px;
height: 20px;
left: 10px;
```

```
z-index: 10;
font-family: verdana, helvetica, sans-serif;
font-weight: bold;
font-size: 12px;}

.submenu
{position: absolute;
left: 25px;
width: 120px;
border: 1px solid black;
background-color: yellow;
layer-background-color: yellow;
font-family: verdana, helvetica, sans-serif;
font-size: 10px;
visibility: hidden;}
</STYLE>

<SCRIPT LANGUAGE="JavaScript">
var nummenus = 3; // Number of menus

var titlearray = new Array(); // An array for the title
objects
var submenuarray = new Array(); // An array for the submenu
objects

if (document.layers) { // Sets visibility for NN and IE
visible = 'show';
hidden = 'hide';
}
else
if (document.all) {
visible = 'visible';
hidden = 'hidden';
}
// Fills the arrays with title and submenu objects
for (var i = 0; i < nummenus; i++) {
titlearray[i] = ('title' + i);
submenuarray[i] = ('submenu' +i);
}
// Changes the image when the menu item is opened
function picopen(n) {
title = ('title' + n);
```

```
pic = ('pic' + n);
if (document.layers) {
document.layers[title].document.images[pic].src =
"opened.gif";
}
else if (document.all) {
document.all(pic).src = "opened.gif";
    }
}
function picclose(n) {
title = ('title' + n);
pic = ('pic' + n);
if (document.layers) {
document.layers[title].document.images[pic].src =
"closed.gif";
}
else if (document.all) {
document.all(pic).src = "closed.gif";
    }
}
function toggle(n,move) {
menu = ('submenu' + n);
if (document.layers) {
submenu = document.layers[menu];
}
else if (document.all) {
submenu = document.all(menu).style;
}
if (submenu.visibility == visible) {
submenu.visibility = hidden;
picclose(n);
for (var i = (n+1); i < nummenus; i++) {
if (document.layers) {
document.layers[titlearray[i]].top -= move;
document.layers[submenuarray[i]].top -= move;
}
else
if (document.all) {
document.all(titlearray[i]).style.pixelTop -= move;
document.all(submenuarray[i]).style.pixelTop -= move;
    }
}
```

```
}
else {
submenu.visibility = visible;
picopen(n);
for (var i = (n+1); i < nummenus; i++) {
if (document.layers) {
document.layers[titlearray[i]].top += move;
document.layers[submenuarray[i]].top += move;
}
if (document.all) {
document.all(titlearray[i]).style.pixelTop += move;
document.all(submenuarray[i]).style.pixelTop += move;
    }
  }
}
lastmenu = submenu;
}
</SCRIPT>
</HEAD>

<BODY>

<DIV CLASS="title" ID="title0" STYLE="top: 0px">
<A HREF="#" onclick="javascript: toggle(0,30); return
false"><IMG NAME="pic0" SRC="closed.gif" BOR-
DER="0">Bücher</A>
</DIV>

<DIV CLASS="submenu" ID="submenu0" STYLE="top: 20px">

<A HREF="http://www.pearsoned-ema.com/"
TARGET="display">Pearson Education</A><BR>
<A HREF="http://ft.com/"
TARGET="display">FT.com</A>
</DIV>

<DIV CLASS="title" ID="title1" STYLE="top: 20px">
<A HREF="#" onclick="javascript: toggle(1,60); return
false"><IMG NAME="pic1" SRC="closed.gif"
BORDER="0">Business</A>
</DIV>
```

```
<DIV CLASS="submenu" ID="submenu1" STYLE="top: 40px">
<A HREF="http://www.w3c.org/"
TARGET="right">W3 Consortium</A><BR>
<A HREF="http://www.xml-rpc.org/"
TARGET="display">XML-RPC.prg</A><BR>
</DIV>

<DIV CLASS="title" ID="title2" STYLE="top: 40px">
<A HREF="#" onclick="javascript: toggle(2,45); return
false"><IMG NAME="pic2" SRC="closed.gif"
BORDER="0">Search engines</A>
</DIV>

<DIV CLASS="submenu" ID="submenu2" STYLE="top: 60px">
<A HREF="http://www.lycos.co.uk/"
TARGET="display">Lycos</A><BR>
<A href="http://www.uk.yahoo.com/"
TARGET="display">Yahoo</A><BR>
<A HREF="http://www.altavista.com/"
TARGET="display">Altavista</A>
</DIV>

</BODY>
</HTML>
```

The only important thing now is that the two image files `opened.gif` and `closed.gif` are located in the same folder as the `menu.htm` file. The result of this menu should look like this:

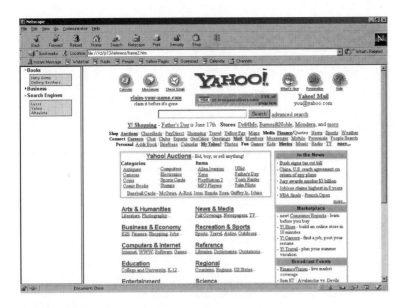

Figure 3.3 *The menu tree appears on the left*

3.3 HTML tags

JavaScript is integrated in HTML documents. For this reason, you should have a general overview of which tags are available in this language. The list of HTML tags includes an explanation of each tag.

> **Tip** Just remember that not every tag works in every browser. We don't have enough space here to deal with the attributes of the individual tags.

3.3.1 Overview of themes

Here you will find a list of all tags sorted according to thematic areas.

HTML structure

`<body>`, `<head>`, `<html>`, `<frameset>`

Head elements

`<base>`, `<isindex>`, `<link>`, `<meta>`, `<nextid>`, `<scripts>`, `<style>`, `<title>`

Hyperlinks

`<a>`

Line breaks

`<br>`, `<nobr>`, `<wbr>`

Paragraph formats

`<address>`, `<blockquote>`, `<center>`, `<cite>`, `<code>`, `<dfn>`, `<h1>`, `<h2>`, `<h3>`, `<h4>`, `<h5>`, `<h6>`, `<marquee>`, `<multicol>`, `<p>`, `<pre>`

Font formats

`<abbr>`, `<b>`, `<big>`, `<blink>`, `<em>`, `<font>`, `<i>`, `<kbd>`, `<q>`, `<s>`, `<samp>`, `<small>`, `<strike>`, `<strong>`, `<sub>`, `<sup>`, `<tt>`, `<u>`, `<var>`

Lists

`<dd>`, `<dir>`, `<dl>`, `<dt>`, `<li>`, `<menu>`, `<ol>`, `<ul>`

Tables

`<caption>`, `<col>`, `<colgroup>`, `<thead>`, `<tbody>`, `<tfoot>`, `<table>`, `<th>`, `<td>`, `<tr>`

Forms

`<button>`, `<fieldset>`, `<form>`, `<input>`, `<keygen>`, `<label>`, `<legend>`, `<optgroup>`, `<option>`, `<select>`, `<textarea>`

Frames

`<frame>`, `<frameset>`, `<noframes>`

Multimedia elements

`<area>`, `<bgsound>`, `<img>`, `<map>`, `<object>`

Embedded objects

`<applet>`, `<embed>`, `<iframe>`, `<noembed>`, `<noscript>`, `<param>`, `<script>`

Revision

`<del>`, `<ins>`

3.3.2   A

`<a>`

The most important tag in HTML is `<a>` because (together with the attribute `href`) it defines a link to other HTML pages or other data. A text area or other object is defined as an anchor for the link.

`<abbr>`

This tag identifies abbreviations. This can be useful when using search engines for example.

`<acronym>`

This tag identifies acronyms. This can be useful when using search engines for example.

`<address>`

This tag is specially intended for framing addresses. The address is then usually indented and displayed in italics.

`<applet>`

This tag allows you to incorporate Java applets. Browsers that support Java ignore all data enclosed by `<applet>` ... `</applet>` except for the `<param>` tag. In contrast, browsers that do not support Java ignore `<applet>` and the enclosed `<param>` tags. They display all other data contained in `<applet>` ... `</applet>`. The same applies if the Java applet causes an error and cannot be loaded.

`<area>`

You need this tag to create client-side image maps. You can create hot areas within these image maps.

3.3.3   B

`<b>`

Text enclosed by `<b>` ... `</b>` appears in bold face.

`<base>`

This tag allows you to specify a basic default setting for `href` and `target` for all HTML elements on the page.

`<basefont>`

This tag sets the default font.

`<bdo>`

This tag stands for "bi-directional override". It is used when an HTML document is to contain languages that read from left to right as well as languages that read from right to left.

`<bgsound>`

This tag allows you to play background music.

`<big>`

Text enclosed in `<big>` ... `</big>` appears in a larger font size.

`<blink>`

This tag is used to make the framed text block flash.

`<blockquote>`

This marks quotations. Quotations are usually indented both left and right.

`<body>`

This tag is responsible for structuring the HTML page at top level. All text and image elements should be enclosed by `<body>` ... `</body>` because global attributes are defined here that affect the whole HTML body.

`<br>`

This tag is used to force a line break.

`<button>`

This tag creates buttons in forms.

3.3.4   C

`<caption>`

You can only use this tag within `<table>` ... `</table>`. This tag shares the same level as `<tr>`. It creates a table heading or caption for the entire width of the table.

`<center>`

This centers a text block together with all other HTML elements.

`<cite>`

This marks quotations. This usually appear in italics.

`<code>`

You can use this tag to format source code. This is usually displayed in a non-proportionate font.

`<col>`

This tag complements conventional tables. This is where you make table column settings. This tag is always contained within a `<colgroup>` ... `</colgroup>` configuration. No data is inserted here as this area is exclusively for formatting.

`<colgroup>`

This tag is used in `<table>` ... `</table>` and only contains `<col>` tags. It is used to allow columns to be formatted before the table data is entered.

`<comment>`

Passages enclosed by `<comment>` ... `</comment>` are recognized as comment by the browser and ignored.

3.3.5   D
`<dd>`

This tag is used within definition lists `<dl>` ... `</dl>` and itself encompasses a definition description. The text is usually left indented.

`<del>`

This allows you to delete text passages and other source code without losing these in the source text. Because the time of deletion is specified, some browsers can display a page in the status corresponding to the time you specify. Other browsers display deleted passages in a different color from the current passages. The remaining browsers just display the current status.

`<dfn>`

This marks definitions and usually displays them in italics.

`<dir>`

This tag creates a list of (usually) short entries. These are separated from each other by `<li>`.

`<div>`

This tag marks a section of a text that is to begin and end with a line break.

`<dl>`

A definition list is created here. This can contain entries of the type `<dd>` and `<dt>`.

`<dt>`

This tag stands for "Definition Term" and is used in definition lists `<dl>`.

3.3.6   E

`<em>`

This marks text to be highlighted. This usually appears in italics.

`<embed>`

This tag is used to incorporate plugin data in the browser. The attributes mentioned above are requested directly from the browser and all others are transferred to the plugin without being processed.

3.3.7   F

`<fieldset>`

Groups together input elements from forms.

`<font>`

This tag is the most powerful font design resource in HTML 4. The attributes affect the font type and size.

`<form>`

A form is created here. All form elements (such as `<input>`) are enclosed by `<form>` ... `</form>`.

`<frame>`

This tag creates a frame within `<frameset>` ... `</frameset>`. The attributes of this tag affect the individual frames.

`<frameset>`

This tag indicates that this page is to create frames. It replaces the `<body>` tag and contains `<frame>` tags as well as other `<frameset>` statements.

3.3.8   H
`<h1>` to `<h6>`

This is where headings are created. `<h1>` produces a first level heading and `<h6>` creates a sixth level heading.

`<head>`

This tag marks the head of an HTML line. The line between `<head>` ... `</head>` contains information about the contents of the document rather than actual document information.

`<hr>`

Produces a horizontal split bar on the screen.

`<html>`

This is the top-level tag in the hierarchy. All other tags are located within `<html>` ... `</html>`. This tag is used to mark the complete HTML code as such.

3.3.9   I
`<i>`

You can use this tag to mark text to appear in italics.

`<iframe>`

This frame is called the inline frame and differs from `<frame>` because it does not need to be incorporated in a `<frameset>` structure. An Internet page is inserted in a given area of the page and is handled by the dimensions as an image inserted using `<img>`.

`<img>`

This tag is the standard method for inserting images, graphics and videos into an HTML page.

`<ins>`

This allows text passages and other source code to be inserted without losing the old version of the source text. Because the time of insertion is specified, some browsers can display a page in the status corresponding to the time you specify. Other browsers display inserted passages in a different color from the old passages. The remaining browsers just display the current status.

`<input>`

This tag is used in forms created with `<form>` ... `</form>`. It creates every conceivable form element.

`<isindex>`

You need this tag for special interactive searches in your HTML document.

3.3.10   K

`<kbd>`

This tag formats the enclosed text so that it is obviously recognizable as keyboard input. The text usually appears in a proportionate font.

`<keygen>`

This tag calculates an encryption code that can be used in forms in Netscape to make data transmission more secure.

3.3.11   L

`<label>`

This tag is used to add a description to form fields. This makes it easier to navigate within forms.

`<legend>`

This tag specifies the name for a `<fieldset>`.

`<li>`

This tag defines a list element. All common list types are used.

`<link>`

This tag is used in the HTML head and indicates a link to a document that is related to the current document. The type of relationship in question is defined in the `rel` attribute.

`<listing>`

This returns the source text one-to-one up to the closing `</listing>` tag.

3.3.12   M
`<map>`

You need this tag to create image maps. It contains the hot areas as `<area>` and the image in `<img>` with set `ismap` attribute.

`<marquee>`

This tag creates a running banner which the user can control.

`<menu>`

This tag works in the same way as `<ul>` but is specially intended for one-line list elements.

`<meta>`

This tag is a universal information mechanism that indicates the contents of the HTML page. For example many search engines use the `<meta>` tag to identify lists of keywords.

`<multicol>`

This tag defines several columns of equal width in which the text is inserted as continuous text.

3.3.13   N
`<nextid>`

This tag used to be required in order to name `<a>` tags.

> **Warning** You should not use this tag any more.

`<nobr>`

This marks a text passage that should not contain automatically generated line breaks.

`<noembed>`

This tag is used within `<embed>` ... `</embed>`. It marks source code that should only be executed if the browser cannot process the `<embed>` tag.

`<noframes>`

This tag marks source code that should only be executed if the browser cannot process the `<frameset>` tag.

`<noscript>`

This tag marks source code that should only be executed if the browser cannot process the `<noscript>` tag.

3.3.14   O

`<object>`

This tag is a universal multimedia integration tag.

`<ol>`

This tag creates an ordered (numbered) list.

`<optgroup>`

You can use this tag to group together several `<option>` tags in a selection field and to give them a hierarchy.

`<option>`

This specifies the various options for a selection field.

3.3.15   P

`<p>`

This creates a paragraph.

`<param>`

This tag is responsible for transferring parameters to embedded object (`<object>`, `<applet>` ...).

`<plaintext>`

Here the following text is displayed one-to-one on the screen. Even a closing `</plaintext>` tag is ignored.

`<pre>`

This tag marks preformatted text. All blanks, tabs and line breaks also appear on the screen.

3.3.16   Q

`<q>`

This tag indicates short quotes. The browser inserts quotation marks.

3.3.17   R

`<rt>`

This tag is used within `<ruby>` ... `</ruby>`. It creates the help text for its content.

`<ruby>`

This marks a short piece of text in order to assign a brief explanation to it with `<rt>`. This explanation appears in smaller letters above the content of `<ruby>` ... `</ruby>`. This mechanism was specially introduced for oriental languages in order to provide pronunciation guidelines. You can also use it for purposes of your own.

3.3.18   S

`<s>`

Displays the enclosed text in strike-through form.

`<samp>`

Formats a text as an example. Usually displayed in Courier font.

`<script>`

The `<script>` tag identifies script languages. JavaScript is an example of a script language. This is why we use `<script>` to distinguish JavaScript text from HTML source code.

`<select>`

Specifies a selection list whose elements are defined with `<option>`.

`<small>`

Indicates that the enclosed text is to be displayed in a smaller font.

`<spacer>`

This tag creates an empty placeholder to enable more convenient intermediate spaces to be placed in HTML documents.

`<span>`

This tag is used to perform style sheet formatting directly in the HTML source text. This is useful if CSS can be used to assign a format that could not be resolved in HTML.

`<strike>`

Displays the enclosed text in strike-through form.

`<strong>`

Highlights the enclosed text (usually with bold face).

`<style>`

This tag is called in the head of an HTML page and offers a number of different ways for inserting style sheets in the HTML page.

`<sub>`

Displays the enclosed text as subscript.

`<sup>`

Displays the enclosed text as superscript.

3.3.19 T

`<table>`

This tag defines a table.

`<tbody>`

This defines the body of a table.

`<td>`

This defines a datacell in a table.

`<textarea>`

This defines a text area in a form.

`<tfoot>`

This defines the foot of a table.

`<th>`

This defines the header cell in a table.

`<thead>`

This defines the head of a table.

`<title>`

This defines the title of the HTML page in the HTML head.

`<tr>`

This defines a line in a table.

`<tt>`

This displays the enclosed text in Courier font.

3.3.20 U
`<u>`

This underlines the enclosed text.

`<ul>`

This defines an unsorted list (enumerated list).

3.3.21 V
`<var>`

Formats a text so that it is recognizable as a variable name (usually in italics).

3.3.22 W
`<wbr>`

Tells the browser where a word can be hyphenated. This does not necessarily mean that the word will be hyphenated at this place.

3.3.23 X
`<xml>`

This tag is used to incorporate XML text in an HTML document.

`<xmp>`

The following text appears one-to-one on the screen. The closing `</xmp>` tag halts this mode again.

3.3.24   !
`<!-- -->`

Text enclosed in `<!-- ... -->` is recognized by the browser as comment and ignored.

3.4 Some interesting pages on the web

At this point I'd like to draw your attention to a number of very interesting Internet pages relating to HTML 4 or to this book.

3.4.1   Browsers

Microsoft Internet Explorer

Microsoft Internet Explorer is the most widely used browser. You can download new versions or find out about new plugins and updates here.

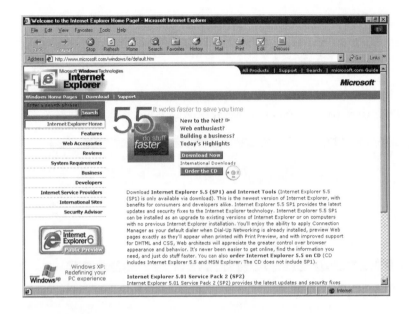

Figure 3.4 *www.microsoft.com/windows/ie*

Netscape Navigator

The second most popular browser is Netscape Navigator. Here you can also obtain updates and further information.

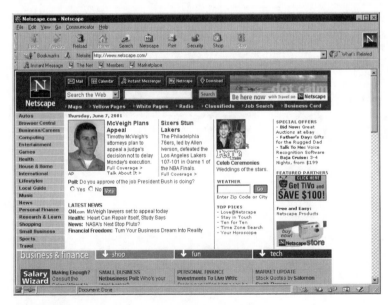

Figure 3.5 *www.netscape.com/*

3.4.2 HTML

Here is a list of interesting pages on the topic of HTML.

W3C

The World Wide Web Consortium (W3C) is responsible for the further development of HTML. Here you will find new references and similar material.

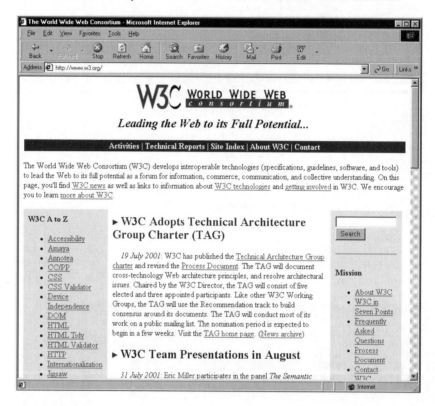

Figure 3.6 *www.w3.org/*

HTML Made Really Easy

If you want a good guide to learning HTML and to some other web related technologies then check out HTML Made Really Easy.

Figure 3.7 *www.jmarshall.com/easy/html/*

Developer Zone

In Developer Zone you will find a lot of useful information on HTML, XML and CSS.

Figure 3.8 *www.projectcool.com/developer/*

WebCoder

If you are looking for references or examples of Dynamic HTML or JavaScript then you should check out WebCoder.

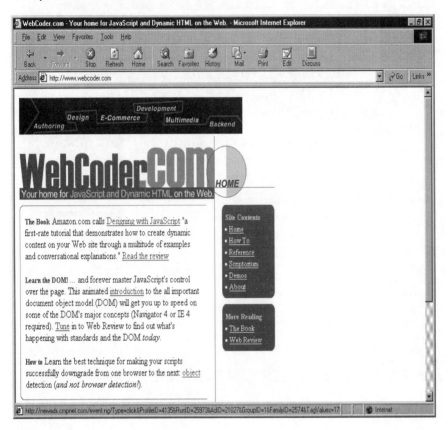

Figure 3.9 *www.webcoder.com*

Site Experts

Site Experts deals with HTML, XML and CSS. It is well worth a visit.

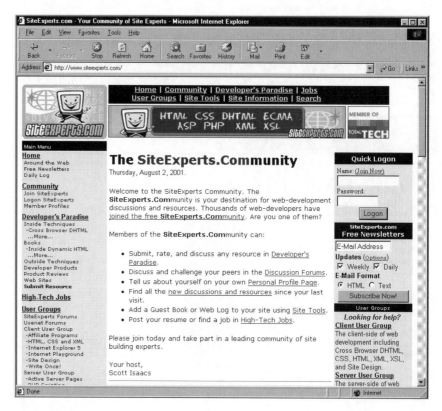

Figure 3.10 *www.siteexperts.com*

3.4.3   About this book

Addison-Wesley

This book is published by Addison-Wesley which has, of course, its own website within Pearson Education's IT-MINDS.COM. Here you will find textbooks written by professionals for professionals.

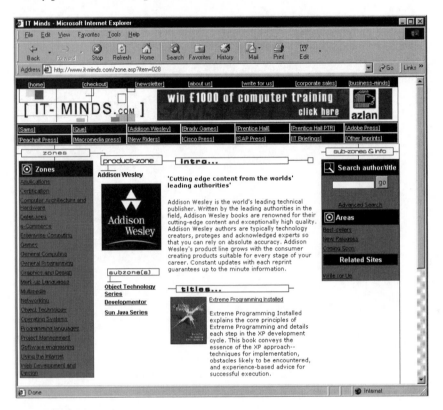

Figure 3.11   *http://www.it-minds.com/*

Appendix

A Character references for special characters

Character	Reference
	
"	"
&	&
<	<
>	>
@	@
{	{
}	}
~	~
¡	¡
¢	¢
£	£
¤	¤
¥	¥
©	©
	¬
®	®
°	°
±	±
µ	µ
¼	¼
½	½
¾	¾
¿	¿
À	À

Character	Reference
Á	Á
Â	Â
Ã	Ã
Ä	Ä
Å	Å
Æ	Æ
Ç	Ç
È	È
É	É
Ê	Ê
Ë	Ë
Ì	Ì
Í	Í
Î	Î
Ï	Ï
Ñ	Ñ
Ò	Ò
Ó	Ó
Ô	Ô
Õ	Õ
Ö	Ö
Ø	Ø
Ù	Ù
Ú	Ú
Û	Û
Ü	Ü
Ý	Ý
Þ	Þ
ß	ß
à	à
á	á
â	â
ã	ã
ä	ä
å	å
æ	æ
ç	ç
è	è

Character	Reference
é	é
ê	â
ë	ë
ì	ì
í	í
î	î
ï	ï
ð	ð
ñ	ñ
ò	ò
ó	ó
ô	ô
õ	õ
ö	ö
ø	ø
ù	ù
ú	ú
û	û
ü	ü
ý	ý
ÿ	ÿ

B

B Predefined color values

Table A.2 lists all predefined colors in JavaScript with their RGB values.

Color	Red	Green	Blue
aliceblue	F0	F8	FF
antiquewhite	FA	EB	D7
aqua	00	FF	FF
aquamarine	7F	FF	D4
azure	F0	FF	FF
beige	F5	F5	DC
bisque	FF	E4	C4
black	00	00	00
blanchedalmond	FF	EB	CD
blue	00	00	FF
blueviolet	8A	2B	E2

Color	Red	Green	Blue
brown	A5	2A	2A
burlywood	DE	B8	87
cadetblue	5F	9E	A0
chartreuse	7F	FF	00
chocolate	D2	69	1E
coral	FF	7F	50
cornflowerblue	64	95	ED
cornsilk	FF	F8	DC
crimson	DC	14	3C
cyan	00	FF	FF
darkblue	00	00	8B
darkcyan	00	8B	8B
darkgoldenrod	B8	86	0B
darkgray	A9	A9	A9
darkgreen	00	64	00
darkkhaki	BD	B7	6B
darkmagenta	8B	00	8B
darkolivegreen	55	6B	2F
darkorange	FF	8C	00
darkorchid	99	32	CC
darkred	8B	00	00
darksalmon	E9	96	7A
darkseagreen	8F	BC	8F
darkslateblue	48	3D	8B
darkslategray	2F	4F	4F
darkturquoise	00	CE	D1
darkviolet	94	00	D3
deeppink	FF	14	93
deepskyblue	00	BF	FF
dimgray	69	69	69
dodgerblue	1E	90	FF
firebrick	B2	22	22
floralwhite	FF	FA	F0
forestgreen	22	8B	22
fuchsia	FF	00	FF
gainsboro	DC	DC	DC
ghostwhite	F8	F8	FF
gold	FF	D7	00

Color	Red	Green	Blue
goldenrod	DA	A5	20
gray	80	80	80
green	00	80	00
greenyellow	AD	FF	2F
honeydew	F0	FF	F0
hotpink	FF	69	B4
indianred	CD	5C	5C
indigo	4B	00	82
ivory	FF	FF	F0
khaki	F0	E6	8C
lavender	E6	E6	FA
lavenderblush	FF	F0	F5
lawngreen	7C	FC	00
lemonchiffon	FF	FA	CD
lightblue	AD	D8	E6
lightcoral	F0	80	80
lightcyan	E0	FF	FF
lightgoldenrodyellow	FA	FA	D2
lightgreen	90	EE	90
lightgray	D3	D3	D3
lightpink	FF	B6	C1
lightsalmon	FF	A0	7A
lightseagreen	20	B2	AA
lightskyblue	87	CE	FA
lightslategray	77	88	99
lightsteelblue	B0	C4	DE
lightyellow	FF	FF	E0
lime	00	FF	00
limegreen	32	CD	32
linen	FA	F0	E6
magenta	FF	00	FF
maroon	80	00	00
mediumaquamarine	66	CD	AA
mediumblue	00	00	CD
mediumorchid	BA	55	D3
mediumpurple	93	70	DB
mediumseagreen	3C	B3	71
mediumslateblue	7B	68	EE

B

Color	Red	Green	Blue
mediumspringgreen	00	FA	9A
mediumturquoise	48	D1	CC
mediumvioletred	C7	15	85
midnightblue	19	19	70
mintcream	F5	FF	FA
mistyrose	FF	E4	E1
moccasin	FF	E4	B5
navajowhite	FF	DE	AD
navy	00	00	80
oldlace	FD	F5	E6
olive	80	80	00
olivedrab	6B	8E	23
orange	FF	A5	00
orangered	FF	45	00
orchid	DA	70	D6
palegoldenrod	EE	E8	AA
palegreen	98	FB	98
paleturquoise	AF	EE	EE
palevioletred	DB	70	93
papayawhip	FF	EF	D5
peachpuff	FF	DA	B9
peru	CD	85	3F
pink	FF	C0	CB
plum	DD	A0	DD
powderblue	B0	E0	E6
purple	80	00	80
red	FF	00	00
rosybrown	BC	8F	8F
royalblue	41	69	E1
saddlebrown	8B	45	13
salmon	FA	80	72
sandybrown	F4	A4	60
seagreen	2E	8B	57
seashell	FF	F5	EE
sienna	A0	52	2D
silver	C0	C0	C0
skyblue	87	CE	EB
slateblue	6A	5A	CD

Color	Red	Green	Blue
slategray	70	80	90
snow	FF	FA	FA
springgreen	00	FF	7F
steelblue	46	82	B4
tan	D2	B4	8C
teal	00	80	80
thistle	D8	BF	D8
tomato	FF	63	47
turquoise	40	E0	D0
violet	EE	82	EE
wheat	F5	DE	B3
white	FF	FF	FF
whitesmoke	F5	F5	F5
yellow	FF	FF	00
yellowgreen	9A	CD	32

C Form reference

Because JavaScript controls form elements in most cases, we have compiled a short reference guide to the attributes of all form tags for you. The browser compatibility information is also important if you want to create compatible forms for several browsers.

C.1 <button>

Tag/Attribute	2.0	3.0	3.2	4.0	Internet Explorer	Netscape
<button>				X	4.0B1	
accesskey				X	4.0B1	
disabled				X	4.0B1	
name				X	4.0B1	
tabindex				X	4.0B1	
type				X	4.0B1	
value				X	4.0B1	

This tag can create buttons in forms.

accesskey

You can use `accesskey` to define a shortcut for reaching the button. Assign a single letter to the attribute. This will now be executed when you press this key together with the relevant shortcut key. This key can vary, depending on which browser and operating system you use.

disabled

This single attribute causes the button to be identified as inactive and suppresses the button's function.

name

Specifies the name of the button to enable it to be identified when transferred to scripts.

tabindex

Specifies the tab index of the button. Positive values represent the position of the button in the list of objects that can be activated with (⬚). Negative values mean that the button does not occur in the tab index.

type

This specifies which function the button is to perform in the form.

Value	Meaning
button	Defines the button as multifunctional. (A separate script is provided for the button.)
reset	The button deletes the form.
submit	The button submits the form data.

value

Specifies the value of the button to be transferred to the script when activated.

C.2   <fieldset>

Tag/Attribute	2.0	3.0	3.2	4.0	Internet Explorer	Netscape
<fieldset>				X	4.0B2	
align					4.0	

Groups together input elements from forms.

align

Specifies the horizontal alignment within the group.

Value	Meaning
center	The contents are centered.
left	The contents are aligned to the left.
right	The contents are aligned to the right.

C.3   <form>

Tag/ Attribute	2.0	3.0	3.2	4.0	Internet Explorer	Netscape
<form>	X	X	X	X	1.0	1.0
accept				X		
accept-charset				X		
action	X	X	X	X	1.0	1.0
autocomplete					5.0	
enctype	X	X	X	X	1.0	1.0
method	X	X	X	X	1.0	1.0
name				X	3.0B1	2.0
target				X	3.0A1	2.0

A form is created here. All form elements (for example `<input>`) are enclosed by `<form>` ... `</form>`.

accept

Specifies the MIME formats that the form may send so that the script or server can react correctly. These formats are separated by commas.

accept-charset

Specifies the character sets that the form may send. These are separated by commas.

action

Specifies the address of the script or server that is to evaluate the form data.

autocomplete

Switches the autocomplete function on (`on`) or off (`off`).

enctype

Specifies the MIME media type in which the data is to be encrypted when being sent.

method

Specifies how the form is to send the data:

Value	Meaning
post	Here the data is sent directly to the script as a separate datastream.
get	Here the data is appended to the URL and then transferred together with this to the target script.

name

This specifies the name of the form in order to address it by means of scripts and to alter it if necessary.

target

This specifies the target frame in which the result data is to be displayed after the form data has been sent.

C.4   <input>

Tag/Attribute	2.0	3.0	3.2	4.0	Internet Explorer	Netscape
<input type="button">				X	3.0B1	1.0
accesskey				X	4.0B1	
disabled				X	4.0B1	
height						4.0B2
name				X	3.0B1	1.0
tabindex				X	4.0B1	
value				X	3.0B1	1.0
width						4.0B2

This tag is used in forms created with <form> ... </form>. It uses the button value for the type attribute to create a button.

accesskey

You can use `accesskey` to define a shortcut for reaching the form element. Assign a single letter to the attribute. This will now be executed when you press this key together with the relevant shortcut key. This key can vary, depending on which browser and operating system you use.

disabled

This single attribute causes the form element to be identified as inactive and suppresses the element's function.

height

Specifies the height of the button in pixels.

name

Specifies the name of the form element to enable it to be identified by scripts. The value of this attribute is also supplied when parsing the form.

tabindex

Specifies the tab index of the form element. Positive values represent the position of the element in the list of objects that can be activated with (⇥). Negative values mean that the element does not occur in the tab index.

value

Specifies the value returned to the script when this form has been activated.

width

Specifies the width of the button in pixels.

Tag/Attribute	2.0	3.0	3.2	4.0	Internet Explorer	Netscape
`<input type="checkbox">`	X	X	X	X	1.0	1.0
accesskey				X	4.0BI	
checked	X	X	X	X	1.0	1.0
disabled		X		X	4.0BI	
name	X	X	X	X	1.0	1.0
tabindex				X	4.0BI	
value	X	X	X	X	1.0	1.0

This tag is used in forms created using `<form>` ... `</form>`. It uses the `checkbox` value for the `type` attribute to create a checkbox.

accesskey

You can use `accesskey` to define a shortcut for reaching the form element. Assign a single letter to the attribute. This will now be executed when you press this key together with the relevant shortcut key. This key can vary, depending on which browser and operating system you use.

checked

This single attribute specifies that the form element is to be activated in the form default setting.

disabled

This single attribute causes the form element to be identified as inactive and suppresses the element's function.

name

Specifies the name of the form element to enable it to be identified by scripts. The value of this attribute is also supplied when parsing the form.

tabindex

Specifies the tab index of the form element. Positive values represent the position of the element in the list of objects that can be activated with (). Negative values mean that the element does not occur in the tab index.

value

Specifies the value returned to the script when this form has been activated.

Tag/Attribute	2.0	3.0	3.2	4.0	Internet Explorer	Netscape
<input type="file">		X	X	X	4.0B2	2.0
accept				X		
accesskey				X	4.0B2	
disabled		X		X	4.0B2	
name		X	X	X	4.0B2	2.0
readonly					4.0B2	
tabindex				X		
value		X	X	X		

This tag is used in forms created with `<form>` ... `</form>`. It uses the `file` value for the `type` attribute to create a file selection field.

accept

Specifies the MIME formats that the form may send so that the script or server can react correctly. These formats are separated by commas.

accesskey

You can use `accesskey` to define a shortcut for reaching the form element. Assign a single letter to the attribute. This will now be executed when you press this key together with the relevant shortcut key. This key can vary, depending on which browser and operating system you use.

disabled

This single attribute causes the form element to be identified as inactive and suppresses the element's function.

name

Specifies the name of the form element to enable it to be identified by scripts. The value of this attribute is also supplied when parsing the form.

readonly

This single attribute specifies that the content of this form element may not be changed by the reader of the page.

tabindex

Specifies the tab index of the form element. Positive values represent the position of the element in the list of objects that can be activated with (⇥). Negative values mean that the element does not occur in the tab index.

value

Specifies the value returned to the script (in other words the file name).

Tag/Attribute	2.0	3.0	3.2	4.0	Internet Explorer	Netscape
`<input type= "hidden">`	X	X	X	X	1.0	1.0
`name`	X	X	X	X	1.0	1.0
`value`	X	X	X	X	1.0	1.0

This tag is used in forms created with `<form> ... </form>`. It uses the `hidden` value for the `type` attribute to create a hidden field which the viewer of the page cannot influence, but which can interact with the script.

name

Specifies the name of the form element to enable it to be identified by scripts. The value of this attribute is also supplied when parsing the form.

value

Specifies the return value to the script.

Tag/Attribute	2.0	3.0	3.2	4.0	Internet Explorer	Netscape
`<input type="image">`	X	X	X	X	1.0	1.0
accesskey				X	4.0B1	
align	X	X	X	X	1.0	1.0
alt				X	4.0B2	4.0
border						1.0
disabled		X		X	4.0B2	
height					4.0B1	1.1
ismap				X		
name	X	X	X	X	1.0	1.0
src	X	X	X	X	1.0	1.0
tabindex				X	4.0B1	
usemap				X		2.0
value	X	X	X	X		
width					4.0B1	1.1

This tag is used in forms created with `<form>` ... `</form>`. It uses the `image` value for the `type` attribute to create an image you can click to submit the form data. It works in the same way as `type=submit`, but also sends the coordinates clicked in the image to the script.

accesskey

You can use `accesskey` to define a shortcut for reaching the form element. Assign a single letter to the attribute. This will now be executed when you press this key together with the relevant shortcut key. This key can vary, depending on which browser and operating system you use.

align

Specifies the alignment of the text that follows the image.

Value	Meaning
middle	The text is aligned centrally on a vertical axis.
left	The text is aligned to the left.
right	The text is aligned to the right.
top	The text is aligned to the top.
bottom	The text is aligned to the bottom.

alt

The value of this attribute is displayed if the browser cannot display images. This is the case with older text browsers for example.

border

Specifies the width of the border that appears around an image. It is given the same color as a normal text link.

disabled

This single attribute causes the form element to be identified as inactive and suppresses the functionality of the element.

height

Specifies the height of the image in pixels.

ismap

This single attribute indicates that hot areas have been defined for this image and that these can be activated by clicking.

name

Specifies the name of the form element to enable it to be identified by scripts. The value of this attribute is also supplied when parsing the form.

src

Specifies the URL of an image that is to be displayed here.

tabindex

Specifies the tab index of the form element. Positive values represent the position of the element in the list of objects that can be activated with ( ). Negative values mean that the element does not occur in the tab index.

usemap

Specifies the address for the client-side image map specifications.

value

Specifies the value returned to the script if this form element has been activated.

width

Specifies the width of the image in pixels.

Tag/Attribute	2.0	3.0	3.2	4.0	Internet Explorer	Netscape
<input type= "password">	X	X	X	X	1.0	1.0
accesskey				X	4.0B1	
autocomplete					5.0	
disabled		X		X	4.0B1	
name	X	X	X	X	1.0	1.0
readonly				X	4.0B1	
tabindex				X	4.0B1	
value	X	X	X	X	1.0	1.0
vcard_name					5.0	

This tag is used in forms created with `<form>` ... `</form>`. It uses the `password` value for the `type` attribute for the password entry line.

accesskey

You can use `accesskey` to define a shortcut for reaching the form element. Assign a single letter to the attribute. This will now be executed when you press this key together with the relevant shortcut key. This key can vary, depending on which browser and operating system you use.

autocomplete

Switches the autocomplete function on (`on`) or off (`off`).

disabled

This single attribute causes the form element to be identified as inactive and suppresses the element's function.

name

Specifies the name of the form element to enable it to be identified by scripts. The value of this attribute is also supplied when parsing the form.

readonly

This single attribute specifies that the content of this form element cannot be changed by the reader of the page.

tabindex

Specifies the tab index of the form element. Positive values represent the position of the element in the list of objects that can be activated with (). Negative values mean that the element does not occur in the tab index.

value

Specifies the value returned to the script.

vcard_name

Specifies a field name for the personal Microsoft visitor's card (vcard). This should be a default value here. The content of this field is only passed on to the recipient of the form data when the form has been submitted.

Value	Meaning
vCard.Business.City	Company address: City
vCard.Business.Country	Company address: Country
vCard.Business.Fax	Company address: Fax number
vCard.Business.Phone	Company address: Phone number
vCard.Business.State	Company address: State
vCard.Business.StreetAddress	Company address: Street and number
vCard.Business.URL	Company address: Homepage address
vCard.Business.Zipcode	Company address: Zip code
vCard.Cellular	Mobile phone number
vCard.Company	Company name
vCard.Department	Department
vCard.DisplayName	Displayed name
vCard.Email	E-mail address
vCard.FirstName	First name
vCard.Gender	Gender
vCard.Home.City	Private address: City
vCard.Home.Country	Private address: Country
vCard.Home.Fax	Private address: Fax number
vCard.Home.Phone	Private address: Phone number
vCard.Home.State	Private address: State
vCard.Home.StreetAddress	Private address: Street and number
vCard.Home.Zipcode	Private address: Zip code

Value	Meaning
vCard.Homepage	Homepage address
vCard.JobTitle	Job title
vCard.LastName	Last name
vCard.MiddleName	Middle name
vCard.Notes	Notes
vCard.Office	Office
vCard.Pager	Pager number

Tag/Attribute	2.0	3.0	3.2	4.0	Internet Explorer	Netscape
`<input type="radio">`	X	X	X	X	1.0	1.0
accesskey				X	4.0B1	
checked	X	X	X	X	1.0	1.0
disabled		X		X	4.0B1	
name	X	X	X	X	1.0	1.0
tabindex				X	4.0B1	
value	X	X	X	X	1.0	1.0

This tag is used in forms created with `<form>` ... `</form>`. It uses the radio value for the type attribute to create a radio button.

accesskey

You can use `accesskey` to define a shortcut for reaching the form element. Assign a single letter to the attribute. This will now be executed when you press this key together with the relevant shortcut key. This key can vary, depending on which browser and operating system you use.

checked

This single attribute indicates that the form element is to be activated in the form's default setting.

disabled

This single attribute causes the form element to be identified as inactive and suppresses the element's function.

name

Specifies the name of the form element to enable it to be identified by scripts. The value of this attribute is also supplied when parsing the form.

tabindex

Specifies the tab index of the form element. Positive values represent the position of the element in the list of objects that can be activated with (⌨). Negative values mean that the element does not occur in the tab index.

value

Specifies the value returned to the script when this form has been activated.

Tag/Attribute	2.0	3.0	3.2	4.0	Internet Explorer	Netscape
<input type="reset">	X	X	X	X	1.0	1.0
accesskey				X	4.0B1	
disabled		X		X	4.0B1	
height						4.0B2
tabindex				X	4.0B1	
value	X	X	X	X	1.0	1.0
width						4.0B2

This tag is used in forms created with <form> ... </form>. It uses the reset value for the type attribute to create a button that can delete the form.

accesskey

You can use accesskey to define a shortcut for reaching the form element. Assign a single letter to the attribute. This will now be executed when you press this key together with the relevant shortcut key. This key can vary, depending on which browser and operating system you use.

disabled

This single attribute causes the form element to be identified as inactive and suppresses the element's function.

height

Specifies the height of the button in pixels.

tabindex

Specifies the tab index of the form element. Positive values represent the position of the element in the list of objects that can be activated with (⌨). Negative values mean that the element does not occur in the tab index.

value

Specifies the value returned to the script when this form has been activated.

width

Specifies the width of the button in pixels.

Tag/Attribute	2.0	3.0	3.2	4.0	Internet Explorer	Netscape
`<input type="submit">`	X	X	X	X	1.0	1.0
accesskey				X	4.0B1	
disabled		X		X	4.0B1	
height						4.0B2
name	X	X	X	X	1.0	1.0
tabindex				X	4.0B1	
value	X	X	X	X	1.0	1.0
width						4.0B2

This tag is used in forms created with `<form>` ... `</form>`. It uses the `submit` value for the `type` attribute to create a button that submits the contents of the form.

accesskey

You can use `accesskey` to define a shortcut for reaching the form element. Assign a single letter to the attribute. This will now be executed when you press this key together with the relevant shortcut key. This key can vary, depending on which browser and operating system you use.

disabled

This single attribute causes the form element to be identified as inactive and suppresses the element's function.

height

Specifies the height of the button in pixels.

name

Specifies the name of the form element to enable it to be identified by scripts. The value of this attribute is also supplied when parsing the form.

tabindex

Specifies the tab index of the form element. Positive values represent the position of the element in the list of objects that can be activated with (⇥). Negative values mean that the element does not occur in the tab index.

value

Specifies the value returned to the script when this form has been activated.

width

Specifies the width of the button in pixels.

Tag/Attribute	2.0	3.0	3.2	4.0	Internet Explorer	Netscape
<input type="text">	X	X	X	X	1.0	1.0
accesskey				X	4.0B1	
autocomplete					5.0	
disabled		X		X	4.0B1	
maxlength	X	X	X	X	1.0	1.0
name	X	X	X	X	1.0	1.0
readonly				X	4.0B1	
size	X	X	X	X	1.0	1.0
tabindex				X	4.0B1	
value	X	X	X	X	1.0	1.0
vcard_name					5.0	

This tag is used in forms created with `<form>` ... `</form>`. It uses the `text` value for the `type` attribute to create a text input field.

accesskey

You can use `accesskey` to define a shortcut for reaching the form element. Assign a single letter to the attribute. This will now be executed when you press this key together with the relevant shortcut key. This key can vary, depending on which browser and operating system you use.

autocomplete

Switches the autocomplete function on (`on`) or off (`off`).

disabled

This single attribute causes the form element to be identified as inactive and suppresses the element's function.

maxlength

Specifies the maximum length of the input text in characters.

name

Specifies the name of the form element to enable it to be identified by scripts. The value of this attribute is also supplied when parsing the form.

readonly

This single attribute specifies that the content of this form element cannot be changed by the reader of the page.

size

Specifies the displayed length of the input text in characters.

tabindex

Specifies the tab index of the form element. Positive values represent the position of the element in the list of objects that can be activated with (⇥). Negative values mean that the element does not occur in the tab index.

value

Specifies the value returned to the script.

vcard_name

Specifies a field name for the personal Microsoft visitor's card (vcard). This should be a default value here. The content of this field is only passed on to the recipient of the form data when the form has been submitted.

Value	Meaning
vCard.Business.City	Company address: City
vCard.Business.Country	Company address: Country
vCard.Business.Fax	Company address: Fax number
vCard.Business.Phone	Company address: Phone number
vCard.Business.State	Company address: State
vCard.Business.StreetAddress	Company address: Street and number
vCard.Business.URL	Company address: Homepage address
vCard.Business.Zipcode	Company address: Zip code
vCard.Cellular	Mobile phone number
vCard.Company	Company name
vCard.Department	Department
vCard.DisplayName	Displayed name
vCard.Email	E-mail address
vCard.FirstName	First name
vCard.Gender	Gender
vCard.Home.City	Private address: City
vCard.Home.Country	Private address: Country
vCard.Home.Fax	Private address: Fax number
vCard.Home.Phone	Private address: Phone number
vCard.Home.State	Private address: State
vCard.Home.StreetAddress	Private address: Street and number
vCard.Home.Zipcode	Private address: Zip code

Value	Meaning
vCard.Homepage	Homepage address
vCard.JobTitle	Job title
vCard.LastName	Last name
vCard.MiddleName	Middle name
vCard.Notes	Notes
vCard.Office	Office
vCard.Pager	Pager number

C.5   *<keygen>*

Tag/Attribute	2.0	3.0	3.2	4.0	Internet Explorer	Netscape
<keygen>						3.0
challenge						3.0
name						3.0

This tag calculates an encryption code that can be used in forms in Netscape to make data transmission more secure.

challenge

This is taken as the basis for the randomly generated code.

name

Specifies the name of the form element to enable it to be identified by scripts.

C.6   *<label>*

Tag/Attribute	2.0	3.0	3.2	4.0	Internet Explorer	Netscape
<label>				X	4.0B2	
accesskey				X	4.0B2	
for				X	4.0B2	

This tag is used to add a description to form fields. This also makes it easier to navigate within forms.

accesskey

You can use `accesskey` to define a shortcut for reaching the marking. Assign a single letter to the attribute. This will now be executed when you press this key together with the relevant shortcut key. This key can vary, depending on which browser and operating system you use.

for

Specifies to which form field this marking is assigned.

C.7   *<legend>*

Tag/Attribute	2.0	3.0	3.2	4.0	Internet Explorer	Netscape
<legend>				X	4.0B2	
accesskey				X	4.0	
align				X	4.0B2	

This tag specifies the name for a `<fieldset>`.

accesskey

You can use `accesskey` to define a shortcut for reaching the legend. Assign a single letter to the attribute. This will now be executed when you press this key together with the relevant shortcut key. This key can vary, depending on which browser and operating system you use.

align

Specifies horizontal alignment within the legend.

Value	Meaning
center	The contents are centered.
left	The contents are aligned to the left.
right	The contents are aligned to the right.

C.8   *<optgroup>*

Tag/Attribute	2.0	3.0	3.2	4.0	Internet Explorer	Netscape
<optgroup>				X		
disable				X		
label				X		

This tag can be used to group together several `<option>` tags in a selection field and to place them in a hierarchy.

disable

This single attribute indicates that this element has been temporarily deactivated.

label

Specifies a short name for the option group.

C.9   \<option>

Tag/Attribute	2.0	3.0	3.2	4.0	Internet Explorer	Netscape
\<option>	X	X	X	X	1.0	1.0
disable		X		X		
label				X		
selected	X	X	X	X	1.0	1.0
value	X	X	X	X	1.0	1.0

Specifies the various options for a selection field.

disable

This single attribute indicates that this element has been temporarily deactivated.

label

Specifies a short name for the option.

selected

This single attribute indicates that this option should be selected in the preferences.

value

This specifies the value for this element to be submitted in the form when this element is selected.

C.10   \<select>

Tag/Attribute	2.0	3.0	3.2	4.0	Internet Explorer	Netscape
\<select>	X	X	X	X	1.0	1.0
accesskey					4.0B1	
align					4.0	
disabled		X		X	4.0B1	
multiple	X	X	X	X	1.0	1.0
name	X	X	X	X	1.0	1.0
size	X		X	X	1.0	1.0
tabindex				X	4.0B1	

Specifies an option list whose elements are defined with `<option>`.

accesskey

You can use `accesskey` to define a shortcut for reaching the selection field. Assign a single letter to the attribute. This will now be executed when you press this key together with the relevant shortcut key. This key can vary, depending on which browser and operating system you use.

align

Indicates the horizontal alignment of the selection field.

Value	Meaning
center	The field is centered.
left	The field is aligned to the left.
right	The field is aligned to the right.

disabled

Indicates that the option list is temporarily deactivated.

multiple

Indicates that more than one option can be selected.

name

Specifies the name of the form element to enable it to be identified by scripts. The value of this attribute is also supplied when parsing the form.

size

Indicates the displayed length of the options in characters.

tabindex

Specifies the tab index of the form element. Positive values represent the position of the field in the list of objects that can be activated with (⬅). Negative values mean that the selection field does not occur in the tab index.

C.11   *<textarea>*

Tag/Attribute	2.0	3.0	3.2	4.0	Internet Explorer	Netscape
<textarea>	X	X	X	X	1.0	1.0
accesskey				X	4.0B1	
cols	X	X	X	X	1.0	1.0
disabled		X		X	4.0B1	
name	X	X	X	X	1.0	1.0

Tag/Attribute	2.0	3.0	3.2	4.0	Internet Explorer	Netscape
readonly				X	4.0B1	
rows	X	X	X	X	1.0	1.0
tabindex				X	4.0B1	
wrap				X	4.0	2.0

Defines a text field in a form.

accesskey

You can use `accesskey` to define a shortcut for reaching the text field. Assign a single letter to the attribute. This will now be executed when you press this key together with the relevant short-cut key. This key can vary, depending on which browser and operating system you use.

cols

Specifies the text columns of the text field.

disabled

This single attribute indicates that this form element has been temporarily deactivated.

name

Specifies the name of the form element to enable it to be identified by scripts. The value of this attribute is also supplied when parsing the form.

readonly

This single attribute specifies that the content of this form element cannot be changed by the reader of the page.

rows

Specifies the text lines in the text field.

tabindex

Specifies the tab index of the text field. Positive values represent the position of the field in the list of objects that can be activated with ( ). Negative values mean that the element does not occur in the tab index.

wrap

Specifies how the lines are to be wrapped.

Value	Meaning
off	The lines are wrapped just as they have been entered. Wrapping does not occur unless (8) is pressed.
soft	The lines are wrapped in the display, but are submitted in the form entered.
hard	The lines are wrapped in the display and are sent to the script in the same way.

D   Conversion of numbers

Dec	Oct	Hex	Dec	Oct	Hex	Dec	Oct	Hex
0	00	0x0	86	0126	0x56	172	0254	0xAC
1	01	0x1	87	0127	0x57	173	0255	0xAD
2	02	0x2	88	0130	0x58	174	0256	0xAE
3	03	0x3	89	0131	0x59	175	0257	0xAF
4	04	0x4	90	0132	0x5A	176	0260	0xB0
5	05	0x5	91	0133	0x5B	177	0261	0xB1
6	06	0x6	92	0134	0x5C	178	0262	0xB2
7	07	0x7	93	0135	0x5D	179	0263	0xB3
8	010	0x8	94	0136	0x5E	180	0264	0xB4
9	011	0x9	95	0137	0x5F	181	0265	0xB5
10	012	0xA	96	0140	0x60	182	0266	0xB6
11	013	0xB	97	0141	0x61	183	0267	0xB7
12	014	0xC	98	0142	0x62	184	0270	0xB8
13	015	0xD	99	0143	0x63	185	0271	0xB9
14	016	0xE	100	0144	0x64	186	0272	0xBA
15	017	x0F	101	0145	0x65	187	0273	0xBB
16	020	0x10	102	0146	0x66	188	0274	0xBC
17	021	0x11	103	0147	0x67	189	0275	0xBD
18	022	0x12	104	0150	0x68	190	0276	0xBE
19	023	0x13	105	0151	0x69	191	0277	0xBF
20	024	0x14	106	0152	0x6A	192	0300	0xC0
21	025	0x15	107	0153	0x6B	193	0301	0xC1
22	026	0x16	108	0154	0x6C	194	0302	0xC2
23	027	0x17	109	0155	0x6D	195	0303	0xC3
24	030	0x18	110	0156	0x6E	196	0304	0xC4
25	031	0x19	111	0157	0x6F	197	0305	0xC5

Dec	Oct	Hex	Dec	Oct	Hex	Dec	Oct	Hex
26	032	0x1A	112	0160	0x70	198	0306	0xC6
27	033	0x1B	113	0161	0x71	199	0307	0xC7
28	034	0x1C	114	0162	0x72	200	0310	0xC8
29	035	0x1D	115	0163	0x73	201	0311	0xC9
30	036	0x1E	116	0164	0x74	202	0312	0xCA
31	037	0x1F	117	0165	0x75	203	0313	0xCB
32	040	0x20	118	0166	0x76	204	0314	0xCC
33	041	0x21	119	0167	0x77	205	0315	0xCD
34	042	0x22	120	0170	0x78	206	0316	0xCE
35	043	0x23	121	0171	0x79	207	0317	0xCF
36	044	0x24	122	0172	0x7A	208	0320	0xD0
37	045	0x25	123	0173	0x7B	209	0321	0xD1
38	046	0x26	124	0174	0x7C	210	0322	0xD2
39	047	0x27	125	0175	0x7D	211	0323	0xD3
40	050	0x28	126	0176	0x7E	212	0324	0xD4
41	051	0x29	127	0177	0x7F	213	0325	0xD5
42	052	0x2A	128	0200	0x80	214	0326	0xD6
43	053	0x2B	129	0201	0x81	215	0327	0xD7
44	054	0x2C	130	0202	0x82	216	0330	0xD8
45	055	0x2D	131	0203	0x83	217	0331	0xD9
46	056	0x2E	132	0204	0x84	218	0332	0xDA
47	057	0x2F	133	0205	0x85	219	0333	0xDB
48	060	0x30	134	0206	0x86	220	0334	0xDC
49	061	0x31	135	0207	0x87	221	0335	0xDD
50	062	0x32	136	0210	0x88	222	0336	0xDE
51	063	0x33	137	0211	0x89	223	0337	0xDF
52	064	0x34	138	0212	0x8A	224	0340	0xE0
53	065	0x35	139	0213	0x8B	225	0341	0xE1
54	066	0x36	140	0214	0x8C	226	0342	0xE2
55	067	0x37	141	0215	0x8D	227	0343	0xE3
56	070	0x38	142	0216	0x8E	228	0344	0xE4
57	071	0x39	143	0217	0x8F	229	0345	0xE5
58	072	0x3A	144	0220	0x90	230	0346	0xE6
59	073	0x3B	145	0221	0x91	231	0347	0xE7
60	074	0x3C	146	0222	0x92	232	0350	0xE8
61	075	0x3D	147	0223	0x93	233	0351	0xE9
62	076	0x3E	148	0224	0x94	234	0352	0xEA
63	077	0x3F	149	0225	0x95	235	0353	0xEB

D

Dec	Oct	Hex	Dec	Oct	Hex	Dec	Oct	Hex
64	0100	0x40	150	0226	0x96	236	0354	0xEC
65	0101	0x41	151	0227	0x97	237	0355	0xED
66	0102	0x42	152	0230	0x98	238	0356	0xEE
67	0103	0x43	153	0231	0x99	239	0357	0xEF
68	0104	0x44	154	0232	0x9A	240	0360	0xF0
69	0105	0x45	155	0233	0x9B	241	0361	0xF1
70	0106	0x46	156	0234	0x9C	242	3062	0xF2
71	0107	0x47	157	0235	0x9D	243	0363	0xF3
72	0110	0x48	158	0236	0x9E	244	0364	0xF4
73	0111	04x9	159	0237	0x9F	245	0365	0xF5
74	0112	0x4A	160	0240	0xA0	246	0366	0xF6
75	0113	0x4B	161	0241	0xA1	247	0367	0xF7
76	0114	0x4C	162	0242	0xA2	248	0370	0xF8
77	0115	0x4D	163	0243	0xA3	249	0371	0xF9
78	0116	0x4E	164	0244	0xA4	250	0372	0xFA
79	0117	0x4F	165	0245	0xA5	251	0373	0xFB
80	0120	0x50	166	0246	0xA6	252	0374	0xFC
81	0121	0x51	167	0247	0xA7	253	0375	0xFD
82	0122	0x52	168	0250	0xA8	254	0376	0xFE
83	0123	0x53	169	0251	0xA9	255	0377	0xFF
84	0124	0x54	170	0252	0xAA			
85	0125	0x55	171	0253	0xAB			

E   Glossary

This is a list of all the terms used in this book that may require further explanation.

Address

All services in the Internet are accessed by means of an address. This can have a variety of formats. An e-mail address might look like this: name@provider.com. A homepage is reached as follows: http://www.provider.com/

Anchor

The image or text you click on in order to reach a page indicated by the relevant link is called an anchor.

Attribute

An attribute can be assigned to a tag in HTML and describes the properties of the element created in greater detail. For example, if you use `<hr>` to create a horizontal split bar, you can define the thickness of the line using the `size` attribute.

```
<hr size=4>
```

This command creates a much thicker line than `<hr>` on its own.

Body

All data, images and other elements that are subsequently to appear in the browser window are listed in the body of an HTML file. The alignment and configuration of these elements is also defined here.

Browser

A browser is a program that transforms HTML language into a graphical image and interprets the user's entries. This enables the user to surf the Internet. The most commonly used browsers are Netscape Navigator and Microsoft Internet Explorer.

CGI

CGI (Common Gateway Interface) is a standard that defines an interface between computers. It is used to define the transfer of data from so-called CGI scripts, for example.

Dedicated line

A permanent link between two computers is called a dedicated line.

Download

Downloading means transferring a file from another computer to your own system.

Dynamic HTML

Dynamic HTML is an extension of HTML that allows you to program animations and lots of other elements with HTML.

Editor

See Text editor.

E-mail

You can use the Internet to send mail. You simply specify the name of the recipient and write your message. In just a few minutes (sometimes even seconds) the recipient will have received your letter as a file. This variant is much faster than normal mail and doesn't even cost the price of a stamp. A letter like this is called e-mail.

FTP

In the context of the Internet, FTP stands for "File Transfer Protocol". Computers communicate with each other in a variety of languages (protocols). This one was specially developed for exchanging data in the Internet. FTP allows you easy access to large file archives belonging to businesses, universities or other institutions.

Guest access

Many service providers supply software to their subscribers. To ensure that this software can only be accessed by subscribers, a prompt appears requesting the user ID and the password when the connection is being set up. Some data is also open to Internet users who are not subscribers. These people can log on under the name "Anonymous". In most cases there is no need to enter a password. However in some cases the guest's e-mail address is expected as the password. You will receive adequate advance warning of this.

Hard disk

A computer stores both the operating system as well as other programs on a hard disk. This hardware is comparable with a floppy disk, but much faster and larger.

Hardware

A computer's hardware consists of the processor itself with all its cards, the monitor, the keyboard, the mouse, the printer and all the other devices connected to it.

Head

The head of an HTML file contains the page title, among other things.

Homepage

A homepage often consists of several files that can be viewed by any Internet user. A homepage is mostly written in HTML language and displayed using a browser program. Homepages contain information about individuals, businesses, universities and other institutions.

HTML

HTML, or Hypertext Markup Language, was developed to make it as easy as possible to create homepages. It regulates the programming of links and simplifies the structure of tables, forms and lists. HTML even allows multimedia elements such as videos and music to be used.

HTTP

The Hypertext Transfer Protocol (HTTP) is used to transfer files based on HTML language. Homepages are mostly transferred using this protocol.

Internet

The Internet is a worldwide network of computers. Originally developed by the military to ensure a fully functional communication network even when some computers have failed. In the meantime, it has also become an important medium for businesses and private individuals.

ISDN

Telephone companies offer not only normal analog telephone lines, but also digital ISDN lines. Here the voice is first transformed into digital patterns before being converted back into acoustic signals on the other side. Because programs and files are stored and transferred by digital means, ISDN is a fast option for data transfer.

Java

Programs written in Java are transferred via the Internet and then run on your system. This programming language was specially developed for the Internet.

Link

A link is a connection between two Internet pages. If you activate a link on the current page, you will be taken to the target page.

Memory

To store data you need memory. This can be main memory or hard disk capacity.

Modem

You need a modem to send data over a telephone line. This hardware transforms data into acoustic signals. There is also a modem on the other side which performs the opposite procedure. A modem can therefore translate in both directions.

Network

A network is a group of computers that exchange data with each other. The Internet is an enormous network.

Operating system

After it starts, every computer must call up a basic program that tells it how to react to entries and how to address the hardware. This program is known as an operating system. The most commonly used versions are Windows 95/98/NT/2000, MS-DOS, OS/2, MacOS and Unix.

Pixel

A pixel is the smallest point that can be shown on a screen. If you use a screen resolution of 800x600 pixels, you can display 480,000 pixels.

Protocol

When data is transferred, some protocols can check whether all data has been received or whether it has been altered by interference during transmission.

Server

A server is a computer that stores data in order to make it available to other systems in the network.

Service provider

A service provider forms the link between the customer and the Internet. You dial into your service provider by modem or ISDN and the provider forwards all the data you call up to your computer.

Software

All programs and data that can be stored are called software.

Source text

The text describing an HTML file is called source text.

Special characters

Special characters are all characters except A to Z and 0 to 9.

Surfing

"Surfing" means switching from one Internet page to another.

Style sheet

A style sheet is a template that can be called up in several HTML pages. This saves a lot of work because changes only need to be made to one file.

Tag

An HTML file consists of normal text. To display other elements, you need to be able to differentiate these elements from the text. This is the purpose of tags. Tags appear in parentheses.

Telnet

Telnet is a protocol that allows you to execute or control programs on other systems. This is a text-based protocol.

Text editor

A text editor is used to create and alter text files. The "Notepad" program in Windows is an example.

Upload

The opposite of downloading. In this case you transfer a file from your own computer to another one.

URL

See Address.

VRML

VRML stands for "Virtual Reality Modeling Language". This can be used to represent virtual environments.

World Wide Web (WWW)

The "World Wide Web" is probably the most interesting Internet service because all homepages can be found there.

Index

memory 277
menubar 183
menus 212
method 107
methods 39, 69
MimeType 134
mimeTypes 137
min 133
MIN_VALUE 139
modem 277
modifiers 102
Mosaic 4
moveAbove 121
moveBelow 121
moveBy 121, 183
moveTo 121, 183
moveToAbsolute 121
multiline 153
multimedia elements 8, 224

N

name 70, 86, 89, 105, 107, 112, 115,
   122, 145, 146, 148, 156, 159,
   172, 175, 177, 183, 268
naming conventions 17
NaN 139, 190
native 17
navigator 135
NEGATIVE_INFINITY 139
netscape 138, 144
Netscape Navigator 5, 237
network 277
new 17
next 113
Notepad 6
null 17
Number 138, 191

O

Object 140
objects 38, 69
octal numbers 19
offscreenBuffering 183
onAbort 195
onBlur 195
onChange 196
onClick 196
onDblClick 196
onDragDrop 197
onError 197

onFocus 197
onKeyDown 198
onKeyPress 198
onKeyUp 198
onLoad 199
onMouseDown 199
onMouseMove 200
onMouseOut 200
onMouseOver 201
onMouseUp 201
onMove 202
onReset 202
onResize 202
onSelect 202
onSubmit 203
onUnload 203
open 100, 183
opener 185
operating system 277
operator precedence 23
Option 142
option 268
option list 269
options 159
outerHeight 185
outerWidth 185

P

package 17
packages 143
paddingBottom 170
paddingLeft 170
paddingRight 170
paddings 170
paddingTop 170
pageX 103, 122
pageXOffset 185
pageY 103, 122
pageYOffset 185
paragraph formats 224
parameter transfer 25
parent 185
parentLayer 122
parse 93
parseFloat 191
parseInt 192
password 144
pathname 126, 129
personalbar 185
PI 133

W

watch 142
which 103
while 18, 33
whiteSpace 170
width 101, 103, 116, 158, 171
window 41, 123, 177, 188
windows 58
with 18
World Wide Web see WWW
write 101
writeln 101
WWW 3, 279

X

x 70, 103, 123, 126

Y

y 70, 104, 123, 127

Z

zIndex 123